Old English Roses

IN EMBROIDERY

Old English Roses
IN EMBROIDERY

JANE ILES

Rosa spinosissima   *Tall Scotch Rose*

David & Charles

Dedicated to
Her Majesty Queen Elizabeth The Queen Mother
to mark her love of roses and
her deep appreciation of embroidery

Collection of Roses *This circular motif could be used*
for a small round sachet or cushion.

A DAVID & CHARLES BOOK

Copyright © Text, designs, charts and line
illustrations Jane Iles 1986, 1994
Copyright © Photography David & Charles
1986, 1994
First published 1986
This edition first published 1994

Jane Iles has asserted her right to be identified
as author of this work in accordance with the
Copyright, Designs and Patents Act 1988.

A catalogue record for this book is available
from the British Library.

ISBN 0 7153 0201 9

Typeset by Typesetters (Birmingham) Ltd
and printed in Italy by New Interlitho SpA
for David & Charles
Brunel House   Newton Abbot   Devon

Contents

Introduction

I have always loved flowers, in particular the sweet scent, pure colours and graceful shapes of roses. So, when I came across an old book about roses in the library of the Royal Botanic Gardens, Kew, I was fascinated and inspired by the beautiful drawings within. The book *A Collection of Roses from Nature* by Mary Lawrance shows wonderful old roses, many of which are no longer seen today. Their names themselves were intriguing and the colourful drawings provided me with instant inspiration for the designs in this book.

While studying the drawings I felt I wanted to know more about their creator, Mary Lawrance. With the help of Hilary Morris of Kew Library I was able to discover a little about this eighteenth-century artist.

Mary lived in London quite near Oxford Circus with her parents and gave botanical drawing lessons, charging half a guinea (just over 50p) for a lesson. Her work was regularly exhibited at the Royal Academy of Art where she was well regarded. When *A Collection of Roses from Nature* was published in 1799 it was an instant success and Mary soon found herself in great demand by the nurserymen. They wanted her to record in her simple yet charming style the new varieties of plants and flowers as they were grown. She even has a rose named after her: *Rosa semperflorens minima* 'Miss Lawrance's Rose'. Mary was quite prolific in her work and had two further collections of drawings published, *Sketches of Flowers from Nature* (1801) and *Collection of Passion Flowers Coloured from Nature* (1802).

Today we can look upon Mary Lawrance's drawings with appreciation, knowing that they are also an historic record of many varieties of rose no longer growing. For my part, I have taken a small group of them to use as my starting point. I have created a collection of rose designs for cushions, bed linen, table linen, towels, scented sachets and wall pictures. Most of the designs can be adapted to suit other embroidery techniques, or can be made into different end products; with just a little careful experimentation and adjustment of the instructions, you can produce something totally different and unique which will give pleasure for years to come, just as Mary's drawings have done.

Special Techniques in Embroidery

Methods of finishing embroidery and the techniques for making up the various items on the following pages are given in the instruction text.

This chapter will help you to understand special techniques involved in embroidery which help to produce a perfect finish. At the end of the book I have included some more designs in the 'Garden of Roses'. These are trace-off patterns of motifs which have not yet been worked. You may want to use some of these to create your own embroidery.

You will also have Mary Lawrance's drawings to inspire you. Study the way she has used colour to depict petals, the way she has shaded and blended tones to produce a realistic bloom, and then 'paint' with your needle and thread to produce your own original rose embroidery. You need very few stitches and will find that if you only use the minimum number (perhaps as litttle as two or three) the effect is much more stunning than if you turn your design into a stitch sampler. It is important, however, to choose and use your threads carefully. Ask yourself whether you need a thick or a fine yarn, and again try to restrict the number of colours you use. Your aim is to create, with fabric and thread, an article of beauty that will not only enhance its surroundings but complement its design source, the old-fashioned rose.

Preparing fabrics

It is often a good idea to neaten the edges of your embroidery fabric before you begin, as continual handling of the fabric will cause the edges to fray. If you are going to stretch your fabric on a rectangular frame you may find it unnecessary to neaten the fabric edges, but when working the fabric in a small hoop it will be handled more and therefore benefit from being protected. Allow a little extra fabric when cutting,

approximately 2.5cm (1in), and either oversew by hand or machine zigzag stitch around the raw edges. The cut edges of canvas benefit from being bound with a tape, such as masking tape, as this holds the threads of the canvas in position preventing them from loosening and falling away.

Using a backing fabric

The weight and strength of fine or semi-transparent fabrics may not be sufficient to securely 'hold' embroidery. The easiest and most effective solution is to place a layer of suitable backing fabric behind the top fabric. White cotton or cotton polyester is usually the best as it provides strength but does not add bulk. Sometimes, however, it is more effective to use a double layer of your chosen embroidery fabric, for example if you want to retain the semi-transparent quality of organdie, then use two layers of it to give the extra strength.

To work with a backing fabric on a rectangular frame I find it easiest to stretch and fix the backing fabric over the frame first, and then add the top fabric. However, if you are going to use a hoop or slate frame, it is better to smooth the two layers of fabric together and baste them with diagonal basting stitches, working from the centre to the sides. Try to keep the fabrics smooth upon a flat surface so that they do not wrinkle against each other. After basting, this double layer can then be mounted within the hoop or frame.

Using spray starch

If your chosen fabric is very soft and flimsy and you do not require this quality while working, spray starch will add sufficient stiffness to make stitching a little easier. It will allow you to cut out with accuracy small and intricate shapes and also makes machine stitching much easier.

Following the manufacturer's

instructions, direct the spray starch onto the wrong side of the fabric, and take the precaution of testing a small piece of the same fabric first, to make sure that staining does not occur and that the stiffening is suitable.

Backing with tissue paper

Tracing paper or tissue paper can also be used as a temporary backing to assist machine stitching of fine fabrics, such as when you are stitching round complicated shapes in appliqué work.

Pin the paper backing to the wrong side of the fabric and stitch through fabric and paper together. Gently tear the paper away afterwards.

With experience and practice you will soon become familiar with different fabrics, learning which are enjoyable and successful to use and how best to use them. If in doubt, work a small test piece even if all you are testing is whether you can successfully mount the fabric, for example it may be too stretchy.

A general principle to remember is always work a small sample if you are unsure about the fabric, threads or technique that you are about to use.

Embroidery frames

The use of a frame to hold the fabric taut while working helps to keep an even tension and makes the placing of stitches much easier.

It is important to choose a suitable type of frame. Of course, personal preference will always enter into your choice, but the size and type of fabric to be stretched, the type of embroidery being worked and, of course, the nature of the end product, should also be taken into consideration.

Embroidery hoops or tambour frames

These are used for small pieces of embroidery worked on plain-weave fabrics which will not become permanently distorted when pulled taut within the round or oval frame. There is a good selection of sizes available. Wooden hoops are usually preferred to the rigid plastic hoops – but again, it is a matter of personal preference.

You will probably want to collect several different sizes of hoop so that you can select the most suitable size for the project.

Working with a hoop
To reduce the risk of marking the fabric, wind cotton tape round each ring. This also helps to prevent the fabric sagging and loosening while working.

If the embroidery is larger than the hoop, remove the fabric when an area has been stitched, place the tissue paper or muslin over the embroidery and then put it back in the hoop to work the next area. Cut away the protecting paper or muslin to expose the next area to be worked.

If you stop working for a long period, it is better to release the fabric from the hoop, as this will prevent distortion or marks occurring on the fabric.

Rectangular frames
There are two types of rectangular frame. A simple, stretcher frame is easy to use and effective. The fabric is stretched over the frame and fastened at the edges with staples or drawing pins. Unlike embroidery hoops, fabric fastened into a rectangular frame does not become loose during working.

An old, cleaned picture frame can be used as a substitute for a stretcher frame. You can also quite easily and inexpensively make your own frames, and as with hoops it is very useful to have a selection of several sizes. You will soon find out which sizes are most useful for your own particular needs.

To make a frame
Use lengths of whitewood 2 × 2cm (¾ × ¾in). The corners can be butted or mitred and held together with wood adhesive glue and nails.

Specialist frames
Slate or rotating frames are more expensive, but they can be of great use as they are adjustable and fabric can be stretched very evenly on them. They are useful when working a long thin strip of embroidery, such as a border for a towel (see Cluster Maiden's Blush Rose Towel page 22).

There are luxury frames available which have legs and stand independently and where the angle of the frame can be adjusted. As these frames are expensive to purchase, it is advisable to test one, to make sure it is stable on its 'feet' and comfortable for working.

Single Burnet-leaved Rose *A simple spray that would adapt well to techniques such as shadow work or appliqué.*

Using a G-cramp

A carpenter's G-cramp, also known as a C-clamp, is a great help when you are working with a rectangular frame. The cramp holds the frame firmly to the edge of a table so that you have both hands free to work with, making stitching much quicker and more comfortable for you. Remember to protect the table from the cramp with a small piece of felt or other thick fabric, as the tightening action of the cramp can damage a wooden surface.

Enlarging or reducing designs

When experimenting with the size of a design always ask yourself whether the design is improved or enhanced by its new proportions. If it is made smaller does it become too fussy; if it is made bigger, does it become ugly and coarse? This can often happen but there are occasions when you will need to change the size of your design. You may find that a design has to be shown as a chart of reduced size for the simple reason that at full size it would not fit the page size of the book or magazine.

When a design is shown on a grid or chart it will have a squared background and you will be told how much bigger or smaller to make your new grid. Once scaled up or down, you will then carefully and accurately copy the design to its new size.

If you want to alter the size of a design that does not already have a grid upon it, you can add your own grid to change size. This is done by placing the original design within a box shape and drawing a grid of squares over it (trying to use rounded measurements at all times). Another box is then drawn with the same proportions, but of the required size. Draw the same number of squares within this as in the original box. Copy the design, square by square, onto the new grid, marking where the design lines cross the grid lines. Join up all these marks.

With the availability of photocopiers it is now very easy and quick to alter the size of a design by a precise amount. This allows you to experiment much more freely with the size of a design.

Transferring designs to fabric

There are several ways of transferring designs to fabric and the method you choose will be governed by the type of fabric and also the use of the embroidery when it is finished. You should never use a method which marks the fabric permanently, unless you are sure the embroidery will never be laundered or dry cleaned (for example a wall picture), or the method of marking is indelible and will not 'bleed' at all.

Dark China Rose *This small, circular motif could be used all over a tablecloth, or as a corner decoration on bed linen. It might also be used on a silk head square.*

Templates

For very simple shapes, draw round a card or paper template directly onto the fabric, using a dressmaker's fabric-marking pencil or a coloured crayon of a suitable colour.

Direct tracing

If the fabric is fine and semi-transparent, the design can be traced through the fabric. Using a black fine-tipped felt pen, trace the design onto paper and then place this under the fabric on a flat, hard surface. Smooth the fabric and then tape it to the surface with masking tape. Sharpen your marking pencil to a fine point, and trace the design onto the fabric, drawing as fine a line as possible. Always try to match the colour of pencil with your embroidery threads or fabric so that the traced lines are less likely to be visible when the embroidery is completed.

Dressmaker's carbon paper

This method is used when fabrics are opaque. Choose a carbon paper colour that can be seen on the background fabric but will blend in with the stitches. When using this carbon paper, take care that the pressure of your hand does not make smudges on the fabric.

Spread the fabric smoothly on a hard surface and then position the carbon paper on top, chalked side down. Place the design pattern on top. Draw over the design lines with a sharp pencil or a tracing tool. Type-writer carbon paper should never be used for transferring designs to fabric.

Basting threads

This method is used when either the fabric is too thick or rough-surfaced for any of the other methods, or on occasions when you cannot risk marking the fabric. The main disadvantage of this method is that it is difficult to transfer very fine design details and it is a time-consuming process.

Trace the design onto tissue paper and pin it to the fabric. With fine sewing thread, work small, even basting stitches through the paper and the fabric, following the design lines. Break the tissue paper away from the basting with a pin and carefully remove it from the fabric. Once the embroidery has been com-pleted, the basting threads are un-picked and removed. Only if they have been totally covered by em-broidery stitches are they left on the fabric.

Note Never use a felt-tipped or ball-point pen on fabric unless it is specifi-cally for marking fabric. Remember that if the fabric is permanently marked you are committed to covering that mark in some way. Also, there is always a risk that these marks may run or bleed if the article is laundered. Never use a graphite pencil. If you have done so by mistake then never try to remove the marks with an eraser – a nasty smudge will be left. If you prick your finger and blood spots the fabric, chew a piece of sewing thread and use this to dab off the blood – your saliva removes your own blood marks – but try to remove the mark as soon as it has happened.

Finishing tips

All the projects in this book include instructions for finishing your embroidery and making it into a beautiful household item, such as a cushion or set of bed linen. You should always remember to handle your stitchery with great care so that the fabric remains clean and fresh when you have finished your embroidery. Try not to press the fabric unless it is really necessary. If you do have to do so never press the embroidery on the right side, as it will flatten and spoil the texture and finish of the stitches. Always press on the wrong side, preferably with a steam iron.

If you need to lace your embroidery over a piece of cardboard to make a picture, remember to allow plenty of fabric around each edge of the design area, so there is sufficient to be folded over to the wrong side. Use acid-free cardboard that will not bend easily, and strong button thread that will not break when pulled tightly.

Sometimes you may find that your embroidery has become warped and its shape distorted. You will then have to carefully stretch it back to its correct shape before you can proceed and make the finished article.

Damp-stretching

If fabric or canvas has become distorted during embroidery, it will need to be damp-stretched to get it back into shape.

If a piece of embroidery is to be damp-stretched, be sure that the fabric is colour-fast and pre-shrunk, and that all the threads or yarns used are colour-fast. Check also that your method of marking the design on the fabric was a 'safe' one and that water-soluble colours or felt-tipped pens have not been used to transfer the design. The process of stretching requires that the fabric absorbs moisture and any fugitive colour will seep through and mark the embroidery.

Place several layers of clean, white blotting paper on a wooden surface. Dampen the blotting paper with cold water. Place the embroidery, right side upwards, on the paper. Carefully stretch and pin opposite sides to the wooden surface, using rust-free drawing pins, easing out any distortion and encouraging the fabric to return to its original shape. Once pinned, the embroidery should be allowed to dry naturally. Remove the pins to release the fabric from the wooden surface. If the embroidery is still distorted, repeat the process.

Care of embroidery

With the use of good quality fabrics and threads your embroidery will last for years, but there are many ways of prolonging the life of the embroidery.

Never place it in strong sunlight or near to very bright artificial lights, as both the heat and the light will cause the colours to fade and the fibres of the fabric and threads to weaken.

Heat and damp will also cause damage, and laundering, ideally kept to a minimum, should be done by hand with great care. Remember never to iron over the right side of your stitchery, use a steam iron on the wrong side.

You may think it is better to store a cherished piece of embroidery away from any possible harm, but do not hide it away – enjoy it. If you do have to store your embroidery for a long period it is best stored flat or rolled smoothly (right side out), in layers of protective, acid-free tissue paper. Then it should be placed in a clean fabric cover such as a pillowcase, and finally placed in a cardboard box or somewhere dark, dry and, of course, moth-free.

Collection of Roses Tablecloth

The design for this beautiful table linen has been almost directly taken from the original drawing for the frontispiece of Mary Lawrence's book. Many of the original components can be identified but some of the flowers and leaves have been omitted to make the design suitable for stitchery. A tablecloth such as this could be an heirloom in the making, handed down from mother to daughter, and something to be treasured for years to come.

The circlet pattern, on pages 14–15, can be adapted for other embroidery techniques and, as an example of what can be done in adapting patterns, a chart for working the design in needlework on canvas, or Cross stitching on evenweave fabric, can be seen on page 17.

Stitches
Chain stitch, Straight stitch, Seeding and French Knots.

Materials required
Finished size: 2m (2¼yd) diameter tablecloth
6 napkins 40cm (16in) diameter
2.50m (2¾yd) of 228cm (90in) white poly/cotton sheeting
Anchor stranded embroidery cotton:
   4 skeins each of 253 (pale apple green); 214 (smoky green); 281 (sage green); 256 (dark apple green)
2 skeins each of 265 (grass green); 60 (pale mauve-pink); 303 (deep golden yellow); 297 (sunshine yellow)
1 skein each of 892 (pale smoky pink); 895 (dark smoky pink); 42 (dark cyclamen); 52 (bright pink);
11 (pale brick); 307 (deep gold); 300 (buttermilk); 301 (deep buttermilk); 1 (white)
white sewing thread

Preparation
Trace the circlet and separate motif patterns on pages 14–15.

Fold the sheeting in half, matching selvedges. Cut 50cm (20in) from one end across the width and put aside for the napkins. Fold the remaining sheeting in half again. From the fold point, measure, pin and mark an arc 100cm (39in) away. Cut along the arc through all layers of fabric, to give a circle of fabric.

Finger-press the folds at the centre to mark the middle of the cloth.

Place the circlet pattern under the cloth fabric and trace the design, using appropriately-coloured fabric-marking pencils. Trace the single flower motifs round the cloth a distance from the circlet to suit your table, spacing them equidistantly.

Preparing the napkins
Cut a circle of paper 42cm (16½in) diameter and use the pattern to cut six napkins from the reserved strip of fabric. Trace a single flower motif onto each napkin so that the flowers point from the centre to the edge.

Neaten the edges of the napkins and the tablecloth by working a scalloped machine-stitched edge, 1cm (⅜in) from the cut edges, using white sewing thread. trim the excess fabric away with trimming scissors. (Alternatively, turn a narrow, machine-stitched hem.)

Working the embroidery
The key on this page is a guide to the colours used for the embroidery.

Key
253 – light side of thick stems, buds
214 – darker side of thick stems, buds
281 – leaves and stems
256 – leaves and stems
265 – leaves and stems, centre circlet
60 – centre pink roses, border, napkins
303 – outer edge yellow rose, inner edge orange-red rose
297 – inner edge, yellow roses
892 – outer edge pink/white rose
895 – thicker stems' thorns
42 – outer edge, dark red roses

52 – centre dark rose, small single
     roses, pink rose
11 – outer edge, orange-red rose
307 – stamens, pistil, orange-red
     rose
300 – outer edges, yellow/white
     rose
301 – pistils, stems, all roses
1 – inner edges, yellow and pink
     roses

Trace-off pattern for the circlet; join the two sections matching the design lines

14

*Trace-off pattern
for the single motifs*

Use three strands of embroidery thread throughout this design. A 20cm (8in) diameter embroidery hoop is recommended.

Working from the picture and using the key as a guide, work all the design lines in Chain stitch. The thicker stems are worked as two lines of Chain stitches, side by side, and tiny Straight stitches are worked at intervals to represent the thorns.

The areas enclosed by Chain stitch, such as the leaves and petals, are built up by working Seeding stitch inside the shapes, using different shades of thread to create a subtle effect and to generally add texture to the design.

The pistils and stamens of the roses are worked in French Knots at the centre, with Straight stitches radiating from them. Clusters of French Knots represent the anthers.

Use the same colourings and stitches to work the single motif.

Finishing

Press the cloth and napkins on the wrong side to remove creases from the fabric and to 'emboss' the stitchery.

Collection of Roses Chair Seat

This design for canvas needlework is based on the frontispiece from Mary Lawrance's book (see page 12). The chart on this page will make an embroidery 33cm (13in) square, which can be used for a stool top or for a chair seat. If you want to work a larger piece of canvas, or a different shape, work more of the background around the circlet.

You can also enlarge the design by working the stitches over more threads of canvas, or by choosing a canvas with fewer threads per cm (to the inch).

Stitches
Tent stitch.
Note: Half Cross stitch can be used if the panel is intended for a wall panel or picture. Roughly half the yarn quantities will then be used.

Materials required
Evenweave canvas 12 threads to 25mm (1in)
1 skein each of Anchor Tapisserie wool: 8000 (white); 8036 (buttermilk); 9612 (creamy pink); 8458 (dark cherry); 8438 (cherry pink); 8416 (rose pink); 8364 (pale rose pink); 8392 (sugar pink); 8136 (golden yellow); 8132 (buttermilk yellow); 8118 (pale sunshine); 8120 (sunshine yellow); 8238 (pillarbox red); 8164 (flame orange); 8140 (tangerine); 9258 (pale moss); 9074 (pale willow); 9202 (dark sage green); 9214 (sage green); 12 skeins 9252 (light stone – not on chart)

Working the embroidery
Following the chart, work each Tent stitch over one vertical and one horizontal thread.

Key

	8458		8000
	8438		8132
	8416		8118
	8364		8120
	8392		8036
	9612		9252
	8238		9214
	8164		9202
	8140		9258
	8136		9074

Rosa lutea bicolour   *Austrian Rose*

Austrian Rose
Cushion

The Austrian Rose *Rosa lutea bicolour* is known as the 'Austrian Copper'. It is on record as having originated as a bud mutation before 1590 but it often reverts back to the typical yellow species of *Rosa lutea* and *Rosa foetida*, which are sometimes known as 'Austrian Yellow' roses. All modern yellow and orange garden roses are derived from this variety.

Interpreting the rose into an embroidery has had to be carefully done because the colours of the rose are so vibrant that any fussiness in stitchery would tend to produce a muddled effect thus, only two stitches are used for the petals.

Stitches

Satin stitch, Roumanian Couching, Long and Short stitch, Straight stitch, French Knots and Back stitches.

Materials required

75cm (30in) of 90cm (36in) cream, lightweight silk fabric
45cm (18in) of 90cm (36in) white cotton fabric for backing
45cm (18in) square cotton fabric
1 skein each DMC stranded embroidery cotton: 921 (rusty orange); 922 (paler rusty orange); 437 (sandy-gold); 738 (pale tangerine); 727 (pale golden yellow); 725 (mid-golden yellow); 726 (sunshine yellow); 504 (pale, smoky green); 503 (smoky green); 472 (pale sage green); 471 (sage green)
1 skein DMC coton perlé No 5 pale cream 745
cream sewing thread
33cm (13in) diameter cushion pad

Preparation

Trace the embroidery pattern on page 17 on tracing paper.

Cut two 45cm (18in) squares from the silk fabric. Reserve one for the back of the cushion. Press any creases from the piece for the cushion face. Place the silk over the tracing and weight the edges. Make certain the design is centred on the fabric.

Using a fabric-marking pencil, carefully trace the design onto the silk. Cut the piece of white backing fabric in half to give two squares. Reserve one for the back of the cushion. Place the other on a flat surface. Place the silk fabric on it, right side up, and matching fabric edges. On top, place the square of cotton fabric. Smooth all the layers flat. Slip the inner ring of a 30cm (12in) diameter embroidery hoop under this 'sandwich' of fabric, making sure that the layers do not move out of position, then put the outer ring in place on top checking to see that the area to be embroidered is within the hoop. With sharp-pointed scissors cut into the centre of the top, protecting, fabric. Do not cut into the silk. Cut a cross in the protecting fabric from the centre to the edges so that the fabric can be folded back to expose the traced design on the silk.

(Placing a piece of fabric over silk, or any pale-coloured fabric, within a hoop is a worthwhile precaution as there is always the risk of the embroidery fabric being soiled around the hoop edge in working.)

Working the embroidery

Use three strands of embroidery thread throughout this design.

The leaves are worked in Satin stitch, laying the threads across the leaf from the edge to the central vein line. There are five stems with leaves. Choose a combination of two of the green thread colours and work the leaves in the two tones. Similarly, use the two green tones to work two close lines of Back stitches to form the curving stems, taking one of the lines up the leaf to the leaf tip. The slightly more sturdy stems leading to the rose buds and flowers have been created with arched lines of Roumanian Couching which gives a raised effect. Choose shades of green for a balanced effect.

Work the base of the buds and the sepals in Satin stitch, using the curves to guide the direction of stitching.

Work the small petals of the rose buds in a combination of the very pale tangerine, sandy-gold, mid-golden yellow and pale golden yellow. Satin stitch has been used to build up the shape and shading of the petals, but where the shapes have tonal changes, a mixture of encroaching Satin stitch and Long and Short stitch are used effectively.

Study Mary Lawrance's drawing and the embroidered cushion and you will see how colour shading can be built up in stitches. You are, in effect, painting with your needle and thread so always consider the direction of each stitch as well as its colour. You may even find it useful to have two needles with different shades of a colour in use at the same time.

Using the same selection of yellow threads, work the undersides of the petals on the two flowers that are seen from the side. The palest colour lies on the edge of the petals and the darkest nearer the hip and stem. Then, using rusty orange, pale rusty orange and sunshine yellow, work the remaining petal shapes of these two roses. Try to create an effect that will make it appear that if you could look down into these roses you would see a bright, yellow centre with tiny stamens, similar to the rose in the centre of the embroidery. The larger petals of the rose in full bloom are also worked in a combination of encroaching Satin stitch and Long and Short stitch while the areas which depict the petals curling over are predominantly rusty orange and pale rusty orange Satin stitch, with tiny, sunshine yellow Straight stitches dispersed along the outer edges to break up the strength of the orange shades.

The stamens which radiate around the centre pistil are worked in pale sage green Straight stitches and tiny pale tangerine French Knots. The pistil is interpreted with a cluster of sandy-gold French Knots.

To complete this embroidery, work the small stamens that appear to be falling away out of the roses with tiny Back stitches and French Knots in the same colours as you used in the open bloom.

Finishing

Remove the embroidery from the hoop. Press the fabric smooth on the wrong side but try to avoid pressing the embroidery itself.

Making up the cushion

On a large sheet of paper draw a 35cm (14in) diameter circle. Cut out the circle for a pattern and place it on the wrong side of the embroidery so that the design is centrally positioned within the circle. Draw around the paper pattern. Baste the two layers of fabric together 1cm (⅜in) from the line. Place the silk and cotton backing fabric circles of the back of the cushion together and prepare to the same stage. Cut out cushion front and back on the drawn line.

Cut the remaining silk fabric into two strips 15×90cm (6×36in). Join these on the short ends with a 1cm (⅜in) seam allowance to make a ring. Press the seam open. Fold the ring along the length, matching the raw edges. Work a double line of gathering stitches along the raw edges.

Pin and baste this frill to the right side of the cushion face, drawing up the gathering threads to fit around the circle, and matching raw edges. Baste the cushion back in position, right sides facing, on the embroidered cushion face. Machine-stitch along the seam lines (1cm (⅜in) seam allowance), leaving a gap in the seam of at least 15cm (6in) for inserting the cushion pad. Clip into the seam allowance to ease the curve. Gently turn the cushion to the right side, trying not to crease the silk fabric.

Insert the cushion pad. Close the open seam with tiny slip stitches.

Making a twisted cord

Cut six pieces of coton perlé 4m (4⅜yd) long. Knot the ends of the six pieces together. Slip a pencil between the threads at each end. With two people each holding a pencil, and keeping the threads tightly pulled, twist the pencils in opposite directions until the threads twist around themselves. Keeping a firm hold of the cord, fold it in half and allow it to twist together, easing it to form an evenly twisted cord.

Sew the cord around the cushion on the seam line, bringing the ends together at centre top. Tie a double knot. Tie knots in the cord ends about 5cm (2in) away, then cut the cord 2cm (¾in) beyond the knots. Tease out the fibres of the threads with a pin or needle so that small tassels are formed.

Trace-off pattern for the Austrian Rose cushion

Rosa alba   *Cluster Maiden's Blush Rose*

Cluster Maiden's Blush Rose Towels

pretty rose involves the use of Buttonhole stitches, worked in scallops, to depict the petals of the full-blown blooms. The same stitch is used in a different way for the leaves.

Stitches
Buttonhole stitch, Stem stitch, Straight stitch and Split stitch.

Materials required
To decorate 1 hand towel and 1 face towel
25cm (10in) of 90cm (36in) white Swiss cotton fabric, with a woven pattern
25cm (10in) of 90cm (36in) white backing cotton fabric
2 skeins each of Anchor stranded embroidery cotton: 48 (pale pink); 49 (very pale pink)
3 strands each of Anchor stranded embroidery cotton: 264 (yellow-green); 214 (smoky-green)
white sewing thread
1 white hand towel 100×56cm (39× 22in), matching face towel

Preparation
Enlarge the towel embroidery pattern from page 25. Trace the smaller face cloth pattern.

From the Swiss cotton, cut a strip 25×60cm (10×24in), and a piece 25×30cm (10×12in). Cut the white backing cotton fabric to the same sizes. (Make any adjustments to the length of the strips to match your own towel if it is of a different size. Allow 2cm (¾in) for turnings.

Place a strip of Swiss cotton over the enlarged pattern. adjust the fabric

The Cluster Maiden's Blush Rose with its pink-tinged petals has been appreciated by rose-lovers for many years. Of European origin, it is believed to have already been available to gardeners by 1797, when Kew Gardens began keeping records.

The interpretation of Mary Lawrance's drawing has been used to decorate bathroom towels. The pattern on page 25 is an example of how a single design can be used as a repeat – in this case, the repeat is a mirror image. The design can be repeated as many times as required and the broken lines indicate where motifs are matched together. The smaller spray on page 24 is used on a matching face towel (see detail this page).

The technique used to interpret this

carefully until you are satisfied with the position of the design, noting that there are two sections of the design on the trace-off pattern and that the third section will be a repeat. If your towel is wider you will use more repeats.

Make sure the dotted guide lines are parallel to the edges of your fabric. When the fabric is in the correct position, trace the design onto the fabric using a fabric-marking pencil.

Place the backing fabric on a flat surface and lay the top fabric over it, matching up the straight edges. Stitch the two layers together with diagonal basting stitches. Place the fabric in a 20cm (8in) diameter embroidery hoop ready to start the embroidery.

Working the embroidery

Use three strands of embroidery thread throughout this design.

Work the blooms in Buttonhole stitch so that the knots of the stitches form the outer edges of each petal. You will find it easier and more effective, if the blooms are worked from their outer edges towards the centres. Use the two shades of pink to depict the texture of the petals, using more of the very pale pink shade on the outer edges and the darker pink where you imagine the colour might be stronger, or shadowed.

Work the stems in Stem stitch using the two green colours. Balance the two shades, working two lines of Stem stitch side by side. The use of a different green for one of the lines will give the thicker stems roundness and shading.

Where the stems form the base of the buds and then grow into the sepals, change the stitching from Stem stitch to Straight stitch, and then into a combination of Split stitch and Straight stitch. You are drawing with your needle and thread so keep your stitches small and try to make them develop into the shapes of the design.

Work the leaves with Buttonhole stitch around the outer edges, using the yellow-green thread. The knots of the Buttonhole stitching should lie on the edge of the leaf, with the bars lying towards the centre vein. The bars should vary in length to give an interesting, textural effect when the inner part of the leaf surface is filled in Straight stitches. Do not place the

stitches too close to one another, as in Satin stitch, but space them evenly. Some of the leaves are seen from the side, so remember that the yellow-green Buttonhole-stitched edge will lie along the centre of the leaf in these instances.

Once the first section of the embroidery has been completed, reposition the fabric in the hoop and work the next section. You may wish to vary the shading of the petals and leaves slightly or you may wish to follow the exact colouring in the first section you have worked; either process will create a pleasing effect.

Finishing

When the border strip embroidery is completed remove the fabric from the hoop and press with a steam iron, on the wrong side, to remove any creases and to encourage an embossed effect on the stitchery.

Turn a 1cm (⅜in) hem to the wrong side on all sides and baste. Position the border strip across one end of the towel, making sure that the ends are parallel. Fold under the two short ends. Pin, baste, and then machine-stitch the strip in position.

Face towel

Prepare the fabric for the face towel in the same way as for the hand towel, and trace the design. Work the embroidery, using the same stitches as those used for the towel border.

When the embroidery is completed, remove the fabric from the hoop and press to remove any creases.

Using the trace-off pattern as a guide, cut a diamond-shaped paper template. Pin the template to the wrong side of the embroidery. Trim away the excess fabric, leaving an allowance of 1cm (⅜in) all round. Press the allowance to the wrong side, so that a sharp-edged diamond results. Remove the template and baste round the fabric diamond.

Pin, then baste and machine-stitch the embroidery to one corner of the face towel.

Other ideas for the design

Several repeat patterns of the main motif could be worked along the edge of a bed sheet, with the smaller motif worked on pillow cases. It would also look charming worked along the hem of curtains, or for a tieback for plain curtains.

Trace-off pattern for the face towel embroidery

Use dotted lines as guides when positioning pattern upon fabric. Do not mark the fabric.

Pattern for the Cluster Maiden's Blush Rose towel border opposite. Enlarge the pattern photographically by 122% so that it is approximately 16.5cm (6½in) wide or enlarge to suit your individual requirements.

Rosa provincialis   *Blush Province Rose*

Blush Province Rose Quilted Cushion

The Blush Province Rose *Rosa provincialis* was of great value to thirteenth-century French apothecaries, where its cultivation has been authenticated. A delicately fragrant powder was obtained from the dried and pulverised petals.

The graceful shape of the blooms has provided a design source for a quilted, silk cushion, worked in subtle colourings. The quilting method used known as English or wadded quilting is worked by 'sandwiching' a layer of polyester wadding between a cotton backing and the top fabric. The 'puffed' quilted effect is achieved with tiny Back stitches worked along the design lines, and through all three layers of fabric.

The beauty of quilting is achieved in neat, even stitching but careful planning in working is also important. Stitchery should be worked outwards from the centre, in order to establish a smooth 'sandwiching' of the layers. If stitching is worked at random points, the puffed effect may become uneven.

To ensure the quilting is even, and to make stitchery more manageable, work this project with the use of a rectangular slate frame.

Stitches
Back stitch.

Materials required
1.15m (1¼yd) of 90cm (36in) dusty pink silk fabric
60cm (24in) of 115cm (45in) firm, white backing cotton
45cm (18in) square of medium-weight Terylene wadding
2 skeins each of DMC coton à broder No 16: 818 (light dusky pink); 761 (darker dusky pink)
2 skeins DMC coton perlé No 5: 818 (light dusky pink)
pale pink sewing thread
40×40cm (16×16in) cushion pad

Preparation
Trace the central, floral design from page 28. Trace the corner motif and complete the lattice design, tracing in the corner flower sprays, to make the pattern for a 40cm (16in) square cushion.

Cut a piece from the silk fabric 42cm (16½in) square and reserve this for the cushion back. Cut a second piece 50cm (20in) square for the cushion face. Reserve the remaining silk fabric for the frill.

Place the cushion face centrally over the drawn lattice and corner flower pattern and trace the design onto the fabric using a fabric-marking pencil. Next, position the fabric over the central, floral design trace-off pattern, aligning it carefully within the centre of the lattice design.

Cut a 42cm (16½in) square of cotton backing fabric and reserve it for the cushion back. Cut a second piece, 54cm (21in) square. Lace two opposite sides of the backing fabric to the webbing of a slate frame, working from the middle of sides to the corners. The fabric should not be too taut in the frame. Place the wadding centrally onto the backing fabric and then the silk, face upwards, on top of the wadding. Smooth the layers carefully removing any wrinkles. Work loose lines of diagonal basting to hold the layers together. The silk fabric is cut larger than the wadding, as fabric is taken up during quilting.

Secure the side edges of the fabrics by lacing them to the sides of the frame. The fabric must not be too tight in the frame or the 'puffiness' of the quilting will not develop.

The fabric is now ready for embroidery.

Working the embroidery
Use a single strand of coton à broder thread throughout the design. Work the stems and leaves in the pale dusty pink thread together with the smaller square of the lattice design (see picture). Work the blooms and the

larger latticed square in the darker dusty pink thread.

With this particular design, which is a combination of straight lines and curved shapes, it is advisable to begin the Back stitching along the narrow, parallel lines of the lattice design. Begin with the innermost lines and carefully smooth the fabric, gently moulding it into shape as you stitch. Each stitch must be made in two movements, passing the needle down from the right side of the fabric to the wrong side and then up through the layers to the surface once more. The stitches must be of equal length and evenly placed. With careful practice, and with the frame resting on the edge of the table, you will find you can use both hands to work the stitchery.

Next, stitch the central flower design and, finally, the four corner sprays. It is important to mould and manipulate the silk fabric whilst stitching to form the gently undulating quilting.

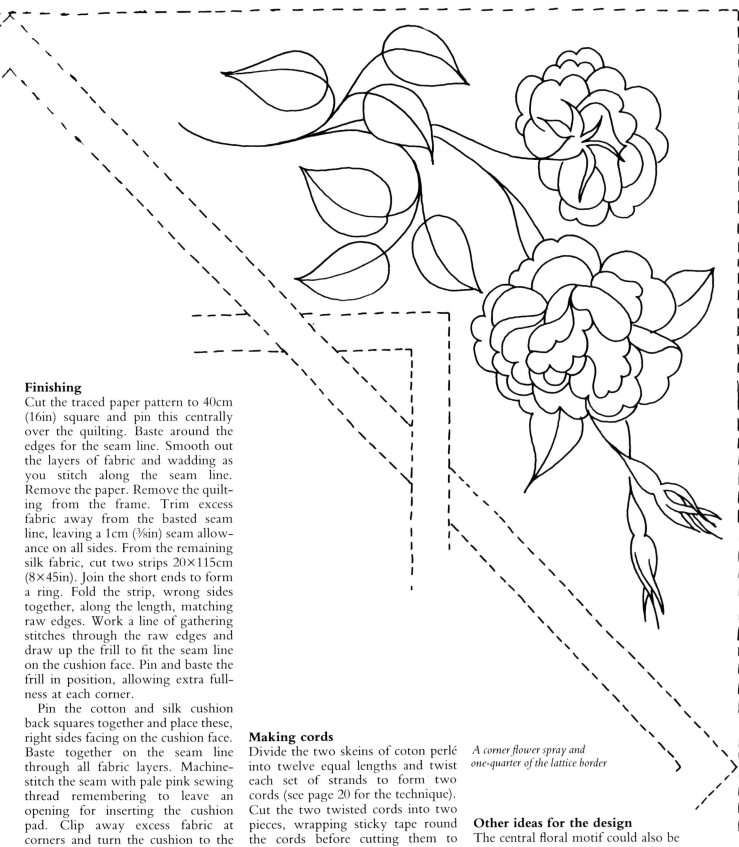

Finishing

Cut the traced paper pattern to 40cm (16in) square and pin this centrally over the quilting. Baste around the edges for the seam line. Smooth out the layers of fabric and wadding as you stitch along the seam line. Remove the paper. Remove the quilting from the frame. Trim excess fabric away from the basted seam line, leaving a 1cm (⅜in) seam allowance on all sides. From the remaining silk fabric, cut two strips 20×115cm (8×45in). Join the short ends to form a ring. Fold the strip, wrong sides together, along the length, matching raw edges. Work a line of gathering stitches through the raw edges and draw up the frill to fit the seam line on the cushion face. Pin and baste the frill in position, allowing extra fullness at each corner.

Pin the cotton and silk cushion back squares together and place these, right sides facing on the cushion face. Baste together on the seam line through all fabric layers. Machine-stitch the seam with pale pink sewing thread remembering to leave an opening for inserting the cushion pad. Clip away excess fabric at corners and turn the cushion to the right side. Insert the cushion pad and slip-stitch the open edges together to close the cushion.

Trace-off pattern for the Blush Province Rose cushion's central motif

Making cords

Divide the two skeins of coton perlé into twelve equal lengths and twist each set of strands to form two cords (see page 20 for the technique). Cut the two twisted cords into two pieces, wrapping sticky tape round the cords before cutting them to prevent them untwisting after cutting.

Sew one cord along each side of the cushion on the seam line. Knot the ends together at the corners. Unravel the threads to make tiny tassels.

A corner flower spray and one-quarter of the lattice border

Other ideas for the design

The central floral motif could also be interpreted into shadow work or shadow quilting. The corner flower sprays would look charming on a pillow slip or worked on the corner of sheets or on napkins and place-mats.

Rosa villosa   *Single Apple Bearing Rose*

Single Apple-bearing Rose Lingerie Case

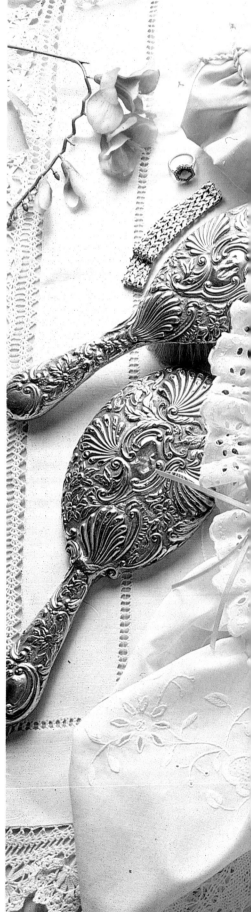

The Single Apple-bearing Rose *Rosa villosa* was first recorded in 1771. Its unusual name apparently arose from the large, round, crimson hips the rose produced, but Mary Lawrance did not include a hip in her drawing.

The clear pink petals and circlet of anthers has been interpreted into a shadow work design for a lingerie case but the pattern could also be used to make a pretty cushion for a day bed.

Stitches
Back stitch and French Knots.

Materials
60cm (24in) of 115cm (45in) pale pink organdie

1.20m (1⅜yd) of 115cm (45in) white cotton fabric

10×15cm (4×6in) piece of bright pink cotton fabric

30×40cm (12×16in) piece of pale green cotton fabric

1m (1⅛yd) of 3mm (⅛in) pink satin ribbon

1m (1⅛yd) of 3mm (⅛in) mint green satin ribbon

3m (3¼yd) of 5cm (2in) gathered broderie Anglaise edging

1 skein of DMC coton perlé No 5 No 16: 742 (yellow)

1 skein of DMC coton à broder No 16: 605 (pale pink)

1 skein of DMC coton à broder No 16: 955 (pale green)

pale pink and white sewing thread

Preparation
Trace the quarter-section of the pattern on page 33 onto a large sheet

of tracing paper. Re-position the tracing paper and trace the section three times, matching the edges, to produce the complete circular design.

With the selvedge edges together, cut the pale pink organdie along the folded edge to give two pieces of fabric.

Cut four pieces of the same size as the organdie from the white cotton fabric.

Reserve one organdie and three white cotton pieces to be used later to make up the lingerie case. Press the remaining fabric carefully. Place the white cotton fabric over the traced pattern. Trace the design using pink and green fabric-marking pencils.

Spray-starch the light green and bright pink fabrics then iron them to stiffen them. (These fabrics must be colour-fast to ensure that their colours do not run if the lingerie case is laundered.) Cut the traced-off pattern to make paper templates of the flowers, leaves and buds. Use the templates to cut shapes from the stiffened fabrics.

Baste each shape in position on the white cotton backing fabric.

Lay the pale pink organdie over the prepared design and work lines of diagonal basting through the fabric layers to hold them together. This design can be worked in a hoop or in the hand.

Working the embroidery
Work Back stitches along the stems and around the leaves and buds using pale green thread. Work Back stitches round the flowers in pale pink thread. Try to achieve an even length of stitch throughout. The delicate circlets of anthers are made with small French Knots.

Finishing
Remove all the basting threads from the finished embroidery. Press the embroidery lightly on the wrong side.

Making the lingerie case
Trace the circle from the pattern on page 33. Use the pattern to cut the embroidery into a circular shape. Cut a circle from the remaining pink fabric and three circles from the white cotton fabric.

Pin and baste the gathered broderie Anglaise edging round the embroidery, matching the edges. Place a white fabric circle under the embroidery and a pink fabric circle on top. Pin, baste and then machine-stitch all round, leaving a gap in the seam of about a quarter of the circumference. Pin, baste and machine-stitch the remaining cotton circles together in the same way to make a lining.

Clip into curves and trim seam allowances. Turn the lining right side out. Put it inside the lingerie case, right sides facing. Match the open seam edges and complete the seam on the case front and partially on the back, leaving a small gap through which the case can be turned. Adjust the lining inside the case and then slip-stitch the open seam. Press the finished case if required.

Make double bows with green and pink ribbons and sew to the case as shown in the picture.

Other ideas for the design
The Single Apple-bearing Rose design makes an ideal embroidery motif for a round tray cloth, worked either in surface stitchery or in appliqué. Circular motifs, such as this, can also be worked effectively in fashion embroidery, perhaps on the back of a light, summer jacket or on the hem of a full skirt.

One-quarter of the Single Apple-bearing Rose
lingerie case pattern; trace the pattern on a
large sheet of tracing paper, then re-position
the paper to complete a circular pattern,
matching the edges of the design

Rosa lutea   *Single Yellow Rose*

Single Yellow Rose Cushion

The Single Yellow Rose *Rosa lutea* originated in Asia Minor, with widespread distribution from Persia to Afghanistan and to the north-west Himalayas. It is one of the few examples in Mary Lawrance's book that is not a pink or white variety. However, it must be remembered that in 1799, when the collection of rose studies was published, there were not the numerous varieties of rose seen in catalogues today.

The Single Yellow Rose has inspired a charming cushion in hand appliqué.

The secret of success in this simple needlework technique lies in the careful and precise preparation of the cut fabric shapes and then the stiches that hold the shapes to the background fabric. Jagged edges and uneven stitchery quickly destroy the embroidery and you will find that time is well spent practising the technique on a sample piece of fabric until you feel confident of undertaking a design.

A few surface stitches are included in the design, but they are kept to the minimum, to emphasise the freshness of the design.

Cotton lawn fabrics in soft colours have been used for the cushion appliqué, two shades of green and two shades of pale yellow. If you have difficulty in purchasing similar soft and subtle colours in lawn, try dyeing your own fabrics. The fabric must be pure cotton and you can use either hot or cold water dyes, mixing colours if necessary until the desired colour is obtained. Rinse dyed fabrics very carefully to remove all traces of dye before embroidery.

Stitches
Buttonhole stitch, Stem stitch, Straight stitch, Chain stitch and French Knots.

Materials required
60cm (24in) of 120cm (48in) cream moiré taffeta fabric
30×60cm (12×24in) piece of pale cream cotton fabric
15cm (6in) squares of cotton lawn in two shades of pale green, two shades of pale yellow
1 skein each of DMC stranded embroidery cottons: 3078 and 745 (pale yellow); 772 and 368 (pale green); 422 (pale brown)
1.50m (1⅝yd) of 3mm (⅛in) lemon yellow satin ribbon
cream, pale yellow, pale green sewing thread to match fabrics
38cm (15in) square cushion pad

Preparation
Trace the pattern from page 36. Trace the appliqué shapes also. Retrace some of the leaf shapes from the main pattern. Place them on the green fabrics and draw round the shapes with a fabric-marking pencil. Cut the petal shapes from the traced patterns (page 37), and use them to cut petals from the yellow fabrics so that each bloom is made up of a combination of both shades of yellow.

Fold the cream fabric to 30cm (12in) square and mount the doubled fabric in a rectangular or square frame.

Place the frame over the main traced-off pattern. The fine lawn fabric will allow you to see the design lines even though the fabric is doubled. Trace the stems and sepals, using a fabric-marking pencil. Position the cut-out fabric leaves and petals on the fabric, using just a touch of water-soluble adhesive, overlapping pieces as necessary. (Look at Mary Lawrance's original study.)

Working the embroidery
Use three strands of embroidery thread throughout this design.

Work neat Buttonhole stitches around all the cut fabric shapes using the appropriate colour thread. Keep stitches small and evenly spaced – they should be quite close together but not as close as for Satin stitch –

Trace-off pattern for the appliqué design

and the knot of the stitch should always lie on the outer edge of the cut fabric shape.

Decide for yourself the shade of green or yellow thread you use. With practise, and gained experience, you will become more discriminating in your use of colour. You will become much more selective when choosing a shade and where you use it. Look carefully at the cushion pictured to help you in your selection.

Work neat lines of tiny Chain stitches to link all the leaves. Build up the thicker, main stem in Chain stitches working lines of each shade of green, side by side.

Where the stems broaden out to become the bulbous buds and sepals, change the stitchery from Chain stitches into Long and Short stitch and Straight stitches.

Add a few Straight stitches along the lower part of the main stem in pale brown to represent the small thorns. Finally, work several small pale brown French Knots in the centre of the full bloom with green Straight stitches radiating out around. Work more small knots around the Straight stitches to complete the stamens. Work a few stamens in the bloom to the right of the full bloom in the same way to complete this embroidered and appliquéd centre panel. Remove the fabric from the frame.

Finishing
Use the broken lined outline on the trace-off pattern on to this page measure and mark out the shape of the embroidered panel section for the cushion. Trim away the excess fabric 1cm (⅜in) from the marked line.

Cut two 40cm (16in) squares of moiré taffeta. From the remaining fabric cut two 10cm (4in) strips across the fabric width.

Centre the embroidered panel on one of the fabric squares. Pin and baste the panel in position. With pale green sewing thread work a decorative machine stitch over the raw edges of the panel. The stitch chosen should entirely cover the cut edges.

Join the short ends of the taffeta strips to make a ring. Use the same decorative machine stitch to neaten one edge. Trim away the excess fabric, close to the line of stitching.

Along the other edge, work a double line of gathering stitches.

Draw up the gathering threads to fit around the seam line of the cushion face. Pin and baste the frill in place matching raw edges. Lay the cushion back, right sides facing, on top. Pin and baste, then machine-stitch on the seam line, leaving an opening along one side large enough to insert the cushion pad.

Clip away excess fabric at the corners and then turn the cushion to the right side. Insert the cushion pad. Turn in the open edges of the seam and close the opening with invisible slip stitches. Cut the satin ribbon into four equal lengths. Tie each length into a bow and hand-sew a bow to each corner of the cushion.

Machine-worked appliqué
This design has been worked totally in hand stitchery. If you prefer, you could apply the fabric shapes with the use of a sewing machine, working round the edges with Satin stitch. This requires a degree of dexterity but, whichever method is chosen, it is vital that the delicacy of the design is maintained.

Trace-off petals for the Single Yellow Rose appliquéd cushion

Rosa carolina   *Single Burnet-leaved Rose*

Single Burnet-leaved Rose Motif

The Single Burnet-leaved Rose *Rosa carolina* was first recorded in North America and, like the Upright Carolina Rose, (page 78), is another species in the Carolinae group. The rose was, apparently, available in England by the time Mary Lawrance produced her book.

The motif abstracted from the original drawings has been used to decorate a soft lid for a basket, and matching handkerchiefs. Another motif is shown on page 9 which could also be used on the basket lid.

Stitches
Fishbone stitch, Stem stitch, Straight stitch, Satin stitch, Long and Short stitch, French Knots and Bullion Knots.

Materials required
35cm (14in) of 90cm (36in) pale pink cotton lawn

35cm (14in) of 90cm (36in) floral cotton

38cm (15in) square of white cotton backing fabric

25×50cm (10×20in) piece of light-weight Terylene wadding

Anchor stranded cotton: 1 skein each 1 (white); 48 (pale pink); 31 (pale tangerine); 933 (pale tan); 240 (light viridian); 472 (light yellow-green)

2 skeins each 62 (bright pink); 264 (light grass green); 206 (light viridian)

pale pink sewing thread

lidded basket, approximately 22cm (8½in) diameter, 8cm (3¼in) deep

3 small coloured cotton handkerchiefs

Preparation
Trace the motifs from pages 40–41. Cut a 26cm (10¼in) square from one

Trace-off pattern for the Single Burnet-leaved Rose motif used on the basket lid

end of the pale pink lawn and place it centrally in a 20cm (8in) diameter embroidery hoop. Position the larger motif pattern underneath the hoop and trace the design using a fabric-marking pencil. Remove the fabric from the hoop and baste it to the white backing fabric. Replace the fabrics in the hoop.

Working the design

Use three stands of embroidery cotton throughout this design. Work the leaves in Fishbone stitch, using different shades of green. Study the picture to see how the tones are balanced. Work the curving stems in Stem stitch. To create a bolder effect, work two lines of stitching side by side, using two different greens. This gives the stems a more rounded effect.

The thorns, along the thicker stems, are worked as Straight stitches in pale tan thread. The small areas of petal exposed between the sepals of the rosebuds are worked in bright pink, using Satin stitch. The petals of the full bloom are worked in a combination of Satin stitch and Long and Short stitch. You will find that you can build up the effect of light and shade on petals if you work inwards, through pale pink, to white in the centre of the bloom.

The smaller rose, viewed from the side, is shaded in a more subtle way, with one petal having a pale pink edge and another fading out to a white edge. Mary Lawrance's drawing will guide you when you are working this particular bloom.

To complete the roses, work a cluster of pale tan French Knots in the centre of the full bloom for the pistil and then, away from the centre, scatter pale tangerine and pale tan Knots for stamens. Similarly, work French Knots on the smaller bloom to represent stamens.

The stylised buds arching over the top of the design and completing the circular shape of the embroidery have green stems in Stem stitch with four tiny Straight stitches across the stem where it thickens to a bud. On either side of the stem, two dainty leaves are worked in Fishbone stitch. The pink buds are built up with three Bullion stitches, worked at right angles to the stem.

Finishing

Remove the embroidered fabric from the hoop. Press on the wrong side to remove the creases if necessary.

Using the pattern as a guide, work basting stitches round the embroidery. Trim excess fabric 1cm (⅜in) from the basted line.

Making the basket lid

Cut and join strips cut from the floral fabric to make a long strip 6cm (2½in) wide by twice the circumference of the embroidery. Join the short ends. Fold the strip, wrong sides facing, matching raw edges and work gathering stitches 6mm (¼in) from the edges. Draw up the gathering to fit round the embroidery.

Pin and baste the frill to the basted seam line, matching raw edges. Cut a circle of the floral fabric to the size of the embroidery and pin and baste it to the right side of the embroidery, sandwiching the frill. Machine stitch all round, leaving a gap in the seam for turning the lid. Turn to the right side. Cut a circle of the wadding and slip it inside the fabric layers. Close the seam with slip-stitches.

The basket can be lined with the remaining fabric, padding it with wadding if desired.

Embroidered handkerchiefs

Place the smaller motif under a corner of a handkerchief, aligning the corner with the dotted guide line. Trace the design through the fabric using a fabric-marking pencil.

Stretch the fabric in a 15cm (6in) diameter embroidery hoop.

Work the embroidery using the same stitches and colour scheme, and with two strands of embroidery cotton.

Trace-off pattern used for the handkerchiefs

Rosa semperflorens　　　　*Dark China Rose*

Dark China Rose Panel

The Dark China Rose *Rosa semper-florens* was discovered by a captain of the British East India Company in 1789. It was the first really dark-coloured rose to be recorded.

The embroidery inspired by this richly-coloured rose is a naively designed appliqué panel. Felt has been used for the simplified flower and leaf shapes and a free-standing appliqué technique has been used. Each shape is finished with an edging of Blanket stitch before being applied.

Printed fabrics have been used for the decorative borders and considerable thought should be given to choosing these. A pattern that is too large or a colour scheme that is too bright will not become part of the overall design but will remain an isolated area.

Stitches
Machine Zigzag stitch, machine Satin stitch, Blanket stitch, French Knots, Chain stitch and Split stitch.

Materials required
60×45cm (24×18in) piece of firm white cotton backing fabric
60×45cm (24×18in) piece of cream cotton lawn
60×45cm (24×18in) piece of olive green/cream lattice print
30×75cm (12×30in) piece of printed cotton in dusky rose
35×25cm (14×10in) piece of printed cotton of closer design in the same colours
35×25cm (14×10in) piece of heavy-weight pelmet interfacing
20×30cm (8×12in) piece of olive green felt
20×30cm (8×12in) piece of dark crimson felt
20×30cm (8×12in) piece of magenta felt
cream sewing thread

1 skein of Anchor stranded cotton:
  307 (golden yellow)
1 skein each of DMC Medicis wool:
  8420 (light green); 8419 (mid-green); 8406 (darker green); 8102 (light crimson); 8103 (dark crimson)

Preparation
Trace the pattern for the panel on pages 44–45. Trace the floral shapes on a second piece of tracing paper. You will be using this to cut templates for the felt shapes.

This panel will be more successfully worked if a rectangular frame is used. If an embroidery frame is not available, you may use a stretcher, or even an old picture frame.

Stretch the white backing fabric on the frame with the cream lawn next and the lattice print on top. You need a working area of at least 38×50cm (15×20in). Using the traced-off pattern and dressmaker's carbon paper, trace the shaped, narrow border onto the pelmet interfacing. Cut out the border and lay it on the wrong side of the smaller piece of dusky pink fabric and baste it in position. Trim the excess fabric from both the inner and outer edges, leaving a 6mm (¼in) turning. Clip into the turning on the curves and across the corner points. Fold the turnings to the wrong side and baste. Top-stitch, using a sewing machine, close to the inner and outer edges, using cream thread.

Fold the larger piece of dusky pink fabric so that it measures 30×37.5cm (12×15in). Spray-starch and iron the fabric – it is easier to handle when it is stiffened.

Trace the zigzag border from the pattern onto the folded fabric using dressmaker's carbon paper.

Pin a piece of tracing paper to the underside of the fabric – this helps to prevent distortion when machine-stitching the zigzags and is easily torn away afterwards.

Set the sewing machine to a wide, close Satin stitch and work along the zigzag lines, using cream thread. Do not stitch the inner border.

Remove the backing paper.

Using very sharp, pointed scissors, cut away the excess fabric round the zigzag stitching and from the inner edge of the border.

Pin the zigzag shape in place making sure that it retains its shape.

Baste in place. Using the inner edge as a guide, cut away the lattice print fabric to expose the cream lawn fabric. Take care at this stage to see that you do not cut into the cream fabric.

Pin the neatened, shaped border in place and slip-stitch to the ground fabrics along the inner edges.

Cut the paper templates from the traced-off pattern and use these to cut out the felt appliqué shapes. You will need 10 small magenta buds, 10 small dark crimson buds, 14 magenta petals (including 5 small petal shapes for the border), 13 dark crimson petals (including 5 large petal shapes for the border), 14 large and 55 small leaves.

Using a single strand of wool, work evenly-spaced Blanket stitches round the edges of all the felt shapes, except the small leaves. Match wool colours to the felt colours as far as possible but when you are working the petals for the two full-blown roses, you should choose wool colours to your own taste – they need not follow a matching scheme. Use the mid- and dark green wools to embroider the larger leaves.

Using the traced-off pattern and dressmaker's carbon paper, trace the stem lines onto the cream fabric background. Arrange the felt shapes on the background before attempting to sew them down. At this stage, your panel is becoming your own interpretation of the Dark China Rose.

Hold the buds in place with a broken circle of small French Knots in the centre of each bud, using two strands of embroidery thread. Work the small leaves with Back stitch veins and work the larger, free-standing leaves in the same way, encouraging them to twist and curl away from the background. Catch the petals down with tiny stitches so that they, too, stand away from the background. Complete the large blooms with a small cluster of larger French Knots in the middle, using six strands of embroidery thread. Work Chain stitch stems using two strands of the mid- and dark green wool to achieve the graceful curves of the design. With a strand of crimson wool and three strands of yellow embroidery thread in the needle together, work small Split stitch thorns. The use of two yarns together produces an interesting effect. Slip-stitch round the outer edge of the plain border with cream thread to complete the embroidery. Remove the panel from the frame. It will need to be mounted before framing.

Trace-off pattern for the Dark China Rose panel; trace the two sections, matching them on the design lines

Rosa alpina   *Alpine Rose*

Alpine Rose Traycloth

The Alpine Rose *Rosa alpina* is of European origin but the exact date of its discovery is unknown. The prettiness of Mary Lawrance's drawing of the pale pink blooms and graceful foliage has been interpreted effectively into a cutwork embroidery design for a traycloth.

The central garland is a simple abstraction of buds and leaves contrasting with the more realistic outer garland of full-blown blossom.

Cutwork is a simple needlework technique but patience and perseverance is needed to achieve success. Not only must the cutting of the fabric be precise, but neatness and uniformity in the stitchery is essential. Once the technique is perfected, you will be encouraged to extend this design, and others in this book, to table and bed linens and, perhaps, to fashion accessories also.

Stitches
Buttonhole stitch, Satin stich, Stem stitch and French Knots.

Materials required
50×60cm (20×24in) piece of pale willow green linen-type fabric
1 skein each of Anchor stranded cotton: 311 (pale gold); 24 (pale pink); 50 (pale rose pink); 60 (pale mauve pink); 216 (willow green); 877 (darker willow)
2 skeins of Anchor stranded cotton: 206 (pale mint green)

Special equipment required
A pair of very sharp, fine-pointed scissors
A stiletto (this is a sharp-pointed tool used to form the hole of an eyelet by piercing the fabric, easing the threads of the fabric apart to form a small hole without breaking them).

If a stiletto is not available, a medium-sized knitting needle can be used instead.

Preparation
Oversew or zigzag machine-stitch the raw edges of the fabric to prevent them from fraying.

Trace the Alpine Rose pattern on pages 48–49 onto one half of a large sheet of tracing paper. Turn the paper and trace the design again, matching the two half-sections accurately.

Transfer the design onto the right side of the fabric using dressmaker's carbon paper, matching the straight grain of the fabric with the grain line on the pattern.

To work this design, the fabric may be held in your hand or stretched in a hoop or frame.

Working the embroidery
Use three strands of embroidery cotton throughout this design. Begin with the stylised rosebud eyelets in the central area of the tray cloth. To make the eyelets, pierce the fabric in the centre of each bud circle and gently ease the stiletto (or knitting needle) backwards and forwards through the fabric to create a small hole. Work small, close buttonhole stitches round the hole, with the knots lying away from the hole. You will find that, as you work, the tension of the stitching encourages the hole to grow slightly bigger and it will naturally form a neat, circular shape. Work the rosebud eyelets in pale pink and pale rose pink threads, alternating colours for each eyelet. Using the pale mint green thread, work the tiny leaves in satin stitch. To produce a slightly raised or embossed effect, Back-stitch round each leaf on the design line, then work diagonal Satin stitch across the shape.

The gently curving stem which links the eyelets and leaves is worked in pale green Stem stitch.

Working the embroidery
The principle of the cutwork technique used in this design is to remember to work all the lines of Buttonhole stitch as evenly and closely-spaced as possible with the knots of the stitches always lying to the outside of the shape being worked, or to the edge which will eventually be cut. This will give a stronger edge when the fabric is cut

away. Using the willow and darker willow green thread, Buttonhole-stitch along the outlines of the leaves, stems and sepals, taking care to reproduce the smoothly flowing curved shapes which are so important to the design.

The fully-opened blooms are worked in a combination of the pale pink and pale rose pink threads. The other blooms, and the eyelets, are worked in pale mauve-pink thread.

Work lines of pale green Stem stitch to form the inner edge of the rose stem.

In the centre of each fully-opened bloom, work a pale gold eyelet. Around the eyelet, work the stamens in pale green Stem stitch and pale gold French Knots.

Finishing
The finished embroidery will probably require careful pressing. Place it right side down on a soft pad of clean fabric and steam press gently to flatten the fabric and encourage the embroidery on the right side to appear more embossed. Spray starch can be used to stiffen the fabric if desired. With very sharp, fine-pointed scissors, snip into the small areas of fabric to be cut away between the leaves, stems and flowers (see the pattern). Cut away these areas of fabric, taking great care not to cut the embroidery threads. Finally, cut away the excess fabric round the entire table mat to outline the finished traycloth.

Sections of this design, such as the rose motifs, could be adapted and used to edge bed linen or for linen towels. The pattern of the roses and leaves is ideal for an appliqué technique, or areas of the design could be used for quilting. Refer to pages 28–29 for the technique.

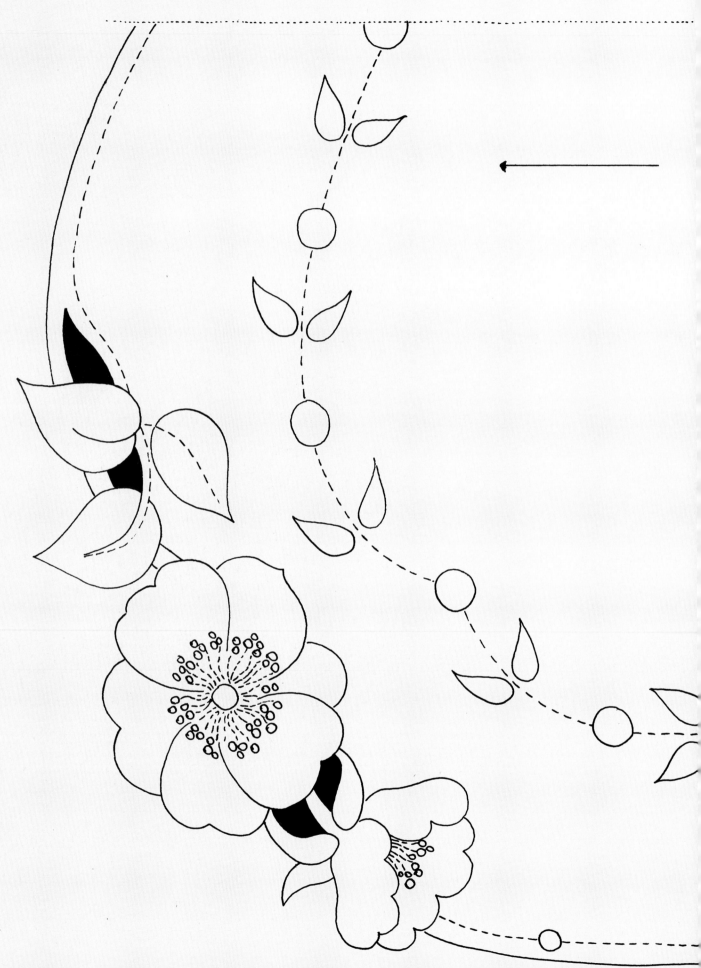

Trace-off pattern for the Alpine Rose tray-cloth; trace the two sections and join them, matching the design lines

Rosa centifolia   *Lisbon Rose*

Lisbon Rose Cushion

The Lisbon Rose *Rosa centifolia*, like the Stepney Rose, is one of the charming group of Centifolias which were developed, mainly in Holland, at the end of the sixteenth century.

The rose has been interpreted into surface embroidery for a panel set into a cushion and edged with ribbon.

Stitches
Long and Short stitch, satin stitch, Overcast stitch, Blanket stitch, Stem stitch and French Knots.

Materials required
50cm (20in) of 150cm (60in) printed cotton fabric

40cm (16in) of 160cm (63in) floral printed cotton fabric

42cm (16½in) square of white cotton backing fabric

42cm (16½in) square of pale green cotton lawn

125cm (50in) of 1cm (⅜in) dusty rose velvet ribbon

2m (2¼yd) of 1cm (⅜in) green velvet ribbon

1 skein each of Anchor stranded embroidery cotton: 48 (very pale pink); 50 (pale pink); 313 (pale tangerine); 264 (pale grass green); 240 (pale apple green); 203 (pale mint green); 225 (mint green); 1 (white)

white sewing thread

cushion pad

Preparation
Trace the embroidery pattern from page 53.

Position the green lawn fabric on the tracing and trace the design with a fabric-marking pencil. Place the lawn on the backing fabric and stretch both fabrics together in an embroidery hoop.

Working the embroidery

Use three strands of embroidery thread throughout this design.

The petals are worked in a combination of Long and Short stitch and Satin stitch. Work the stems in Overcast stitch to produce a raised effect. Vary the angle of the stitches occasionally. Work the leaves in Blanket stitch. Work the anthers in small French Knots in the centre of the full flower. Work the thorns in Split stitch and Stem stitch.

Finishing

Remove the finished embroidery from the hoop and press lightly on the wrong side.

Making up the cushion

Place the embroidery face upwards on a work surface. Cut two 15cm (6in) squares from the floral print. Cut the squares in two diagonally to give four triangles. Position the triangles, right sides up, round the embroidery so that the long edges form a square 'frame' (see picture). Pin, baste and then machine-stitch the triangles to the embroidery, stitching close to the edges.

Cut a 'frame' from the print fabric 7cm (2¾in) deep. Pin and baste the mounted embroidery to the frame.

Machine-stitch the green velvet ribbon over the fabric edges. Cut the ribbon at the corners and then start the next side. Stitch the inner edges first, then the outer edges. At the corners, cut the thread ends to about 30cm (12in). Thread both into a needle and then hand-sew the corners neatly, turning the ribbon ends into a neat mitre.

Machine-stitch the pink ribbon over the edges of the triangular pieces, stitching and finishing in the same way (see picture).

To make the frill, cut two strips of the floral fabric each 10cm (4in) wide across the width of the fabric. Join the short ends and press the seams open.

Work a decorative machine-embroidery stitch along one long edge, 1cm (⅜in) from the edge. Trim away the raw edge with pointed trimming scissors. (If your machine does not have a machine-embroidery facility, hand-roll a narrow hem and hand-sew it.)

Work two rows of gathering stitches along the other long edge of the frill. Gather the frill to fit round the right side of the cushion face, matching raw edges. Pin and baste and then machine-stitch the frill in position, working 1cm (⅜in) from the edge.

Cut the cushion back to the same size as the cushion face. Place the cushion back and face together, right sides together, sandwiching the frill between. Pin, baste and then machine-stitch on three sides and part of the fourth. Turn the cushion to the right side and insert the cushion pad. Fold in the edges of the open seam and close with slip-stitches.

Cut the remaining green velvet ribbon in four pieces. Fold and sew each piece to make a bow. Sew the bows to the corners of the cushion (see picture).

Trace-off pattern for the Lisbon Rose cushion

Rosa rubiginosa   *Manning's Blush Sweet Briar*

Manning's Blush Sweet Briar Tie-back

Manning's Blush Sweet Briar *Rosa rubiginosa* is known to have been in English gardens in the sixteenth century. It has since been greatly hybridised and the rose's fragrance was much sought after when rose growers were striving to produce new variations.

The design inspired by the rose has been planned with the full bloom repeated and the buds and foliage simplified in order to form a garland shape, so that the design fits comfortably into the area required for curtain tie-backs. The design could be used on curtain hems, or coordinated into other room furnishings.

Stitches
Satin stitch, French Knots, Stem stitch and Straight stitch.

Materials required
30cm (12in) of 115cm (45in) pale pink polyester cotton fabric
30cm (12in) of 115cm (45in) white backing cotton
1 skein of Anchor coton perlé No 5: 254 (pale leaf green)
1 skein each of Madeira embroidery floss (new numbers): white; 0613 (pale pink); 0605 (darker pink); 2013 (fawn); 1414 (pale green); 1501 (light mid-green); 1410 (dark mid-green); 1402 (dark green)
2 curtain rings
pale pink sewing thread
pale green sewing thread (matching)

Preparation
Trace the two sections of the tie-back on pages 56–57, matching the section at A-A and B-B.

Fold the pink fabric in half matching the selvedge edges and cut along the fold. Repeat with the white backing fabric.

Transfer the pattern onto the pale pink fabric using dressmaker's carbon paper, making sure the entire tie-back shape is within the area of the fabric. (The arrow on the pattern should align with the straight grain of the fabric.)

Place the pink fabric over the white backing fabric, matching the edges. Baste the fabrics together with lines of diagonal basting stitches. Reserve the remaining pieces of fabric for lining the tie-back.

Place the fabric in a 20cm (8in) diameter hoop and centre the design.

Working the embroidery
Use three strands of embroidery thread for this design except where otherwise instructed.

The white petals of the mature blooms are worked in closely-spaced Satin stitch which radiates from the central area of each bloom. The middle of the rose is worked with a small cluster of tiny, fawn French Knots.

Once the white petals have been worked their even colouring is broken with tiny pale pink Straight stitches, on the inner edges of the petals only, using two strands of embroidery thread.

The stems of the leaves, and the rosebuds, are worked in small Stem stitches. Try to balance the use of the four green shades to achieve a pleasing arrangement of colour and tone. Use the same shades of green used on the stems to lead into the leaves or buds to give continuity to the design.

Work the leaves in two shades of green, one matching the stem and the other to tone, using Satin stitch. This stitch builds up a dense, even area of colour and has a smooth, rich texture. The feathery young leaves towards the ends of the garland are worked in the very pale green thread.

The rosebuds are worked in a combination of small Satin stitches and Stem stitches in green with a few carefully placed darker pink Straight stitches to give the impression of the bud's petals about to emerge. Always use two shades of the green when working buds because they help to create a more realistic effect.

Finishing

When the embroidery is completed, remove the hoop and press the fabric carefully on the wrong side to remove creases, avoiding the embroidered areas if possible. Cut out the tie-back shape from the traced-off pattern, cutting along the solid line. Pin the pattern to the embroidered area and cut out the fabric. Use the same pattern to cut out pink and white fabric shapes from the reserved fabric.

Place the pink shape on the white shape, then place the embroidery right side down on the pink, matching the edges. Pin, baste, and then machine-stitch along the seam line leaving a gap in the seam for turning.

Trim away the excess fabric at the corners and clip into the seam allowance to ease the curves. Press open the seams, then turn the tie-back to the right side. Fold in the raw edges of the opening and close the seam with slip stitches. Press the tie-back on the wrong side to remove any creases.

Using the green coton perlé thread, Buttonhole stitch around the two curtain rings to cover them. Cut a 10m (11yd) length of coton perlé thread and double it. Make a twisted cord using the technique described on page 20. Hand-sew the cord round the edge of the tie-back, tucking the cord ends under neatly. Sew the curtain rings midway along the short ends of the tie-back.

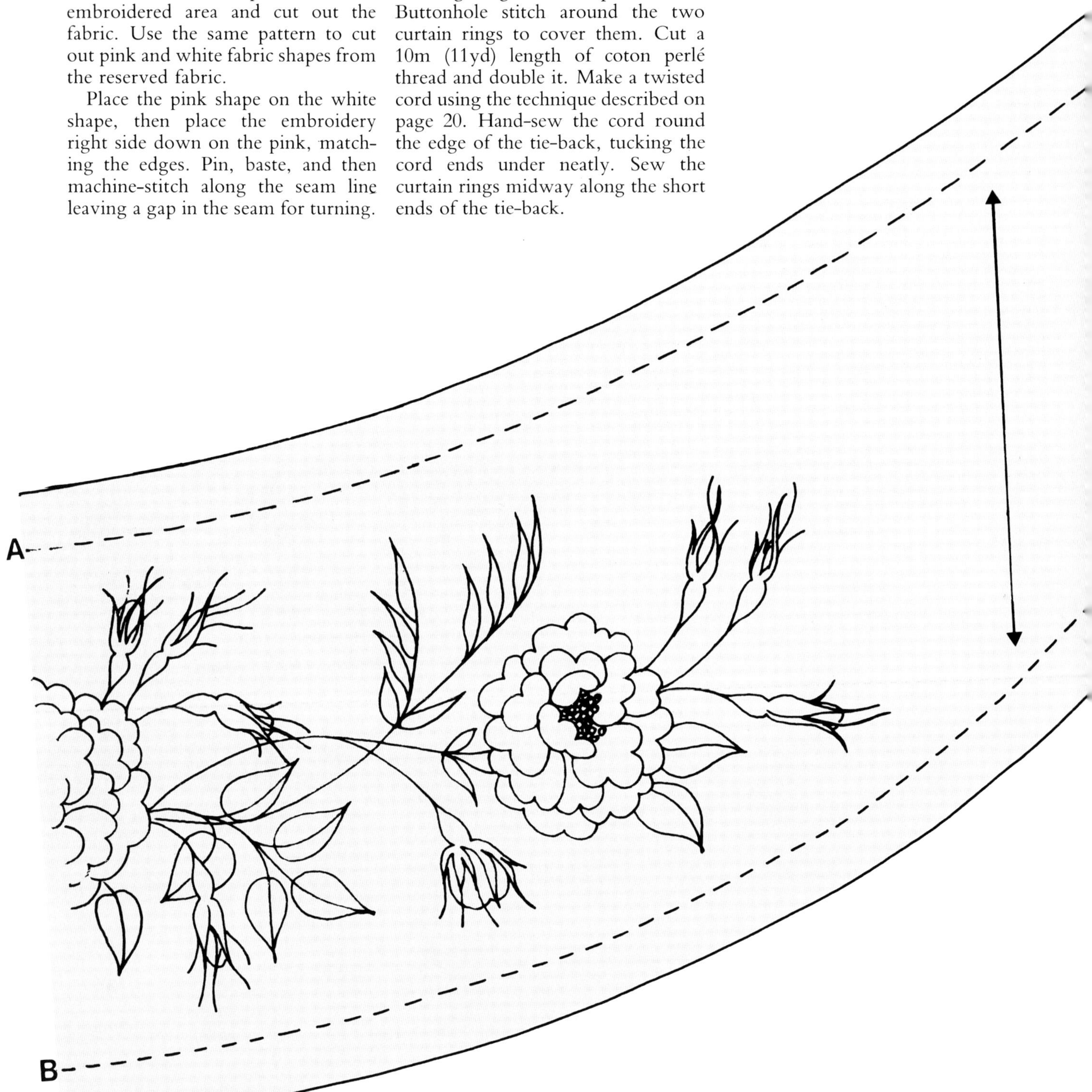

A

B

Trace-off pattern for the Manning's Blush Sweet Briar tie-back; trace the two sections, matching the design lines at A-A and B-B

A

B

Rosa centifolia   *Stepney Rose*

Stepney Rose Table Mats

The Stepney Rose *Rosa centifolia* is another beautiful example of the Centifolias, which first appeared at the end of the sixteenth century. The rose, mainly developed in Holland, was a popular flower with the Dutch Masters of the seventeenth century.

The technique of shadow work has been chosen to interpret the Stepney Rose for a set of table mats. Traditionally, shadow work is worked with white thread on white, semi-transparent fabric. Here, carefully selected colours are used to depict the blooms and foliage and yet the essential delicacy of the embroidery technique has not been lost.

Only two stitches are used, Back stitch to define the scalloped petal edges, and Closed Herringbone stitch. The cross points of the stitches touch each other at the top and bottom of the design line and, on the right side of the work, this produces lines of Back stitches. Stitching must be evenly worked to produce a balanced 'under-shadow' effect and neat regularity on the surface.

Stitches
Back stitch and Closed Herringbone stitch.

Materials required
To make four place mats
2m (2¼yd) of 90cm (36in) white cotton organdie fabric
1 skein each of Anchor stranded cotton: 62 (bright pink); 74 (pale pink); 295 (yellow); 240 (light green); 225 (mid-green); 216 (dark green)
white sewing thread

Preparation
Trace the larger embroidery pattern

on page 60.

Each mat is worked on a double layer of organdie. Cut the organdie into eight 38cm (15in) squares. Reserve the excess fabric.

Place a square of organdie in an embroidery hoop and position the traced-off pattern underneath. Trace the design onto the fabric using green and pink fabric-marking pencils.

On a piece of the reserved fabric, trace off the outlines of the three large roses and the smaller, half-opened bloom. Cut out the shapes.

Remove the organdie from the hoop. Position the piece over a square of organdie, matching edges and the grain lines. Position the cut-out shapes between the two layers, pinning them in place. Place the fabrics in the hoop and adjust the tension screw until the fabric is quite taut. Remove the pins. If the cut-out pieces have moved, you can re-position them with the point of a needle.

Working the embroidery
Use two strands of embroidery thread throughout this design.

Work round the shapes of the full-blown blooms with small Back stitches using pale pink thread. Once the sandwiched shapes are fixed in place, gradually work towards the centres using pale pink thread and then change to the brighter pink. The centre section of each flower is worked in Closed Herringbone stitch to give a suggestion of the colour of the stamens and the pistil. The half-opened bloom is similarly fixed in position with Back stitches using pale pink thread for the larger petals and bright pink for the smaller petals.

The tiny rosebud's petals are outlined in Back stitches using the bright pink thread. Use the dark green thread to work all the thicker stems which wind through the circlet of roses and lead to the blooms and the rosebuds. Use Closed Herringbone stitch for these areas so that neat lines of Back stitches appear on the design lines on the other side of the fabric. Work the leaves in Closed Herringbone stitch also; each leaf is worked in two sections to depict the curve of the centre vein. To add interest to the leaf stems, work them in a line of Back stitches matching the size to those of the Closed Herringbone stitches.

The leaves and stems are worked in light and mid-green threads. Study

Trace-off pattern for the place mat

60

the table mats pictured as a guide to the use of these two shades, working all the leaves that grow from a single stem in the same shade as the stem, and using the other shade for the next group of leaves.

Finishing

Check that the under side of the embroidery is exceptionally neat as any loose ends will show through.

Remove the organdie from the embroidery hoop and carefully press on the wrong side with a steam iron to remove any creases.

Place the embroidery over the traced-off pattern and lightly trace the broken line onto the fabric using a fabric-marking pencil. Work a machine-stitched scalloped edge on the line using white sewing thread. If your sewing machine does not have the automatic embroidery stitch facility, work the edge by hand using Buttonhole stitch and white stranded

cotton. Cut away the excess fabric beyond the finished edge. Work all four mats in the same way.

Glass mats

The smaller trace-off pattern on page 61 is for working a set of matching glass mats. Use the same techniques and stitches as for the place mats. The larger circlet could also be worked in the centre of a table cloth, matching the smaller glass mats in colours. Surface stitches, such as Satin stitch, Long and Short stitch and Stem stitch could be used to interpret the design for this purpose.

Other ideas for the design

The Stepney Rose design, like others in this book, can be worked into Cross stitches, or even into needlework on canvas. Refer to page 84 for the procedure involved in interpreting designs to other needlework techniques.

Trace-off pattern for a glass mat

Rosa damascena   *Blush Damask Rose*

Blush Damask Rose Bed Linen

The Blush Damask Rose *Rosa damascena* is one of the group of roses known as Damasks and is reported to have been in cultivation in Italy in the sixteenth century, Its exact origin, however, is unknown, but its popularity has continued undiminished and Damask roses are still enjoyed by gardeners today.

The beautiful drawing of this pink rose has provided the shapes and colours for an exquisite set of bed linen, worked almost entirely in Back stitch.

Stitches
Back stitch, Straight stitch.

Materials required
1 single bed-sized flat sheet and matching frilled pillowcase
1 10g ball each of DMC coton perlé No 5: white, 818 (pale pink); 776 (deeper pink); 738 (camel); 369 (pale green); 954 (deeper green)

Preparation
Nine repeats of the pattern on pages 64–65 are required to go across the edge of the sheet. The simplest way to achieve these is to have the page photocopied to produce nine separate photostats, which are taped together into a continuous strip. Alternatively, the pattern can be traced onto tracing paper and moved as each repeat is traced. The broken line on the pattern should be aligned with the edge of the sheet.

Lay the pattern on a flat surface and spread the sheet on top. You should be able to see the pattern through the fabric. Pin the sheet to the pattern. Using pink and green fabric-marking pencils, trace the design onto the fabric.

The pillow embroidery requires two repeats. The motifs should be positioned at the end furthest from the opening.

Put the fabric into a 20cm (8in) diameter embroidery hoop, re-positioning the hoop as embroidery progresses.

Working the embroidery
Use one strand of coton perlé throughout this design.

Back stitch is used almost exclusively in the embroidery. Work the leaves and stems in a combination of the two greens balancing the use of them so the effect of light falling on the design from one side is achieved.

Work the rose petals in a combination of pinks, and the centre of the full bloom in camel-coloured thread.

Work the centre pistil as a solid area of several Straight stitches, close together, and then scatter tiny Straight stitches around this to give the effect of stamens.

The colouring of each motif can vary slightly within the colour scheme if you desire, but remember to use the two greens carefully, working them to complement each other.

Use the same basic colour scheme to embroider a matching pillow case.

Finishing
Neaten the wrong side of the embroidery by weaving in all thread ends so that none are left hanging free, spoiling the back of the work. Press the embroidery on the wrong side, over a padded surface, to give an 'embossed' effect to the stitches.

Other ideas for the design
The simplicity of the design could be interpreted as effectively using Chain stitch or Stem stitch, or Coral stitch could be used to provide textural interest on the blooms. Lampshades also lend themselves to embroidered decoration, but make sure thread ends are neatly finished at the back.

The design is eminently suitable for furnishings such as curtains, or it could be worked for a long wall panel. Worked in Satin stitch and Long and Short stitch, the panel could look striking. A single spray, one repeat, abstracted from the design, could be worked on a silk cushion, for a co-ordinated furnishing accessory.

Two repeats of the Blush Damask Rose motif; trace them and link them on the broken design lines

Rosa spinosissima   *Marbled Scotch Rose*

Marbled Scotch Rose
Tablecloth

The Marbled Scotch Rose *Rosa spinos-issima* has been cultivated since ancient times and references in the Herbals of Dodonaens and Gerard show that it was appreciated not only for its beauty but also for its value to the herbalist.

This tiny rose has inspired a simple repeat motif for a tablecloth, worked in Cross stitch and woven ribbon-work. The central motif of four fully-opened roses entwined to form a circle could easily be worked at the corners of a cloth, or just a single motif could be selected.

The use of satin ribbons adds another textural dimension to the embroidery; the ribbon is couched to the fabric with Cross stitches.

The size of the cloth can be adapted to fit your own requirements simply by extending the lines of ribbonwork to the hemline.

Stitches and key

Cross stitch is used throughout this design. On the working chart (page 69) a key is given for the thread colours. Each square of the chart is one Cross stitch worked over two vertical and two horizontal threads. Pink and green ribbons are couched with Cross stitches. For clarity, these couching stitches are shown as black squares. When couching the ribbons, match the thread colour to the ribbon.

Materials

90cm (36in) square of evenweave fabric (12 threads per cm, 30 threads per inch)
4m (4⅓yd) 1.5mm (¹⁄₁₆in) dusty rose satin ribbon
4m (4⅓yd) of 1.5mm (¹⁄₁₆in) willow green satin ribbon
1 skein each of Anchor stranded cotton: 261 (pale olive green); 373 (dark fawn); 313 (pale orange-yellow); 68 (dusty pink)
contrasting basting thread
white sewing thread

Preparation

Neaten the raw edges of the fabric with zigzag machine-stitching or, if you prefer, oversew the edges.

Count the threads, across and down, to find the centre point. Work lines of basting to mark the centre.

This type of embroidery is worked in the hand, without the aid of a frame.

Working the embroidery

Following the chart and key on page 69, work the Cross stitch embroidery using two strands of embroidery thread throughout the design.

Make sure that all the top stitches of the Cross stitches lie in the same direction. Work from the centre of the design, completing the rose motif first, then the border pattern in dark fawn, with a large rosehip in each corner.

Cut the pink and green ribbons to give four lengths of each colour. Couch the green ribbons four threads away from the dark fawn border (see chart). The ribbon is couched with Cross stitches worked at five-stitch intervals. Couch the pink ribbon four threads away from the green ribbon. You can now work the large rose hips in the corners formed by the intersecting ribbons, and work the outer border in dark fawn, with little rose hips spaced along the border. If your cloth is larger than 90cm (36in) square, you will need more ribbon and the dark fawn border and rose-hips will be continued to the edges of the cloth.

Finishing

Unpick the basting threads. Turn and press a doubled narrow hem on the cloth, then hand-hem. As you work, trim the ribbon ends and tuck them into the hem.

If the cloth requires pressing, press on the wrong side, avoiding the embroidered area if possible.

Table napkins

Matching table napkins could be made, following the same design concept. A Cross stitched dark fawn border, with couched ribbons would look attractive or, alternatively, work a single rose from the centre design, with perhaps one or two leaves positioned around it.

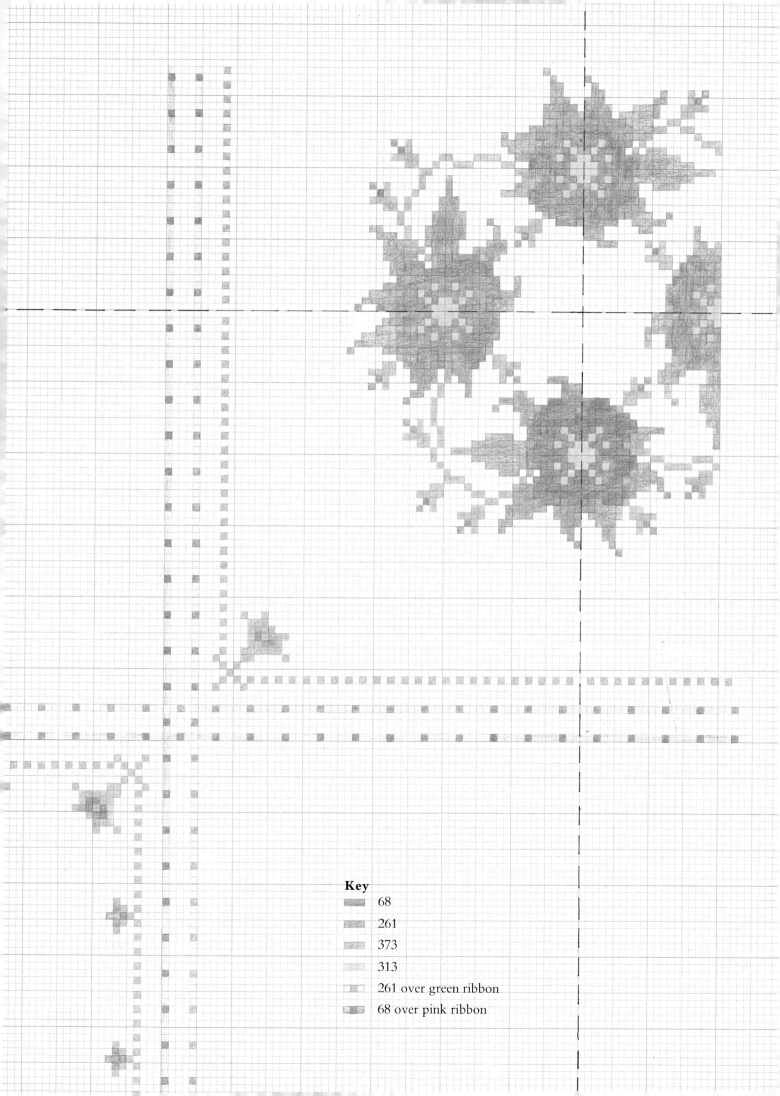

Key

▧	68
▧	261
▧	373
▧	313
▦	261 over green ribbon
▦	68 over pink ribbon

Rosa canina   *Double Dog Rose*

Double Dog Rose Cushion

The Double Dog Rose *Rosa canina* has, in fact, curving teeth-like thorns but there is some doubt that this is the origin of its name. It is suggested in some records that the Romans named the rose Dog Rose because they used a distillation from the roots as a cure for hydrophobia, resulting from a dog bite.

The design for a cushion has been carefully constructed with the circlet of blooms and leaves built up with one spray intertwined with the next. Buds and tiny leaves 'lighten' the edges of the circlet.

This method of design can make a simple motif into an effective component of a complex design.

Stitches
Satin stitch, Long and Short stitch, Stem stitch, French Knots and Straight stitch.

Materials required
45cm (18in) of 90cm (36in) cream, woven wool fabric
45cm (18in) of 90cm (36in) white cotton backing fabric
45cm (18in) of 90cm (36in) white pillow ticking fabric
Terylene cushion filling
1 skein each of DMC Medicis wool: 8514 (pale apricot); 8305 (pale mustard); 8304 (mustard); 8302 (cinnamon)
2 skeins each of DMC Medicis wool: 8407 (dark willow green); 8420 (pale grass green); 8515 (very pale apricot)
3 skeins each of DMC Medicis wool: 8419 (grass green); 8406 (willow green); 8119 (pale mauve-pink); 8111 (pale pink)
1.40m (1½yd) of thin piping cord
1.40m (1½yd) cream, woven binding for piping; cream thread

Preparation
Trace the pattern on pages 72–73 onto a large sheet of tracing paper, re-positioning the paper to draw the other half of the design, making sure that the sprays intertwine correctly. Trace the pattern onto a second sheet of tracing paper, this time using an embroidery transfer pencil.

Cut the wool fabric into two pieces 45cm (18in) square. Cut the cotton backing fabric to the same size. Baste one piece of each fabric, wool and cotton, together. Reserve the remaining pieces.

Following the manufacturer's instructions for using the transfer pencil, transfer the design to the centre of the wool fabric.

Place the mounted wool fabric in a rectangular frame. (An embroidery hoop is not recommended because the size of the design area would mean re-positioning the fabric in the hoop several times and this could easily damage the soft wool fabric.)

Working the embroidery
Use two strands of wool together throughout this design.

Work the leaves in Satin stitch, using different shades of green. Use two darker tones for one group of leaves, then use two lighter tones for the next group. Lay the Satin stitches close together, working from the point of the leaf along one side of the leaf in one shade, then work the other side in the second shade. Stem stitch is used for the thin stems linking the leaves and also for the curving stalks. Where the stems grow into the bases of the rosebuds allow the stitchery to develop into a combination of Satin stitch and Long and Short stitch, mixing shades of green to produce a realistic effect.

The rose blooms are built up with Satin stitch and Long and Short stitches, worked in the dusky pink shades. Use the deeper pink round the outer edges of petals, then build up the remaining area of the petal with the light, and very pale, dusky pink shades.

You are, in effect, 'painting' with yarns, and you should be constantly visualising the effect every stitch is having on the overall design. Stand away from the embroidery occasionally and look at it critically. If a stitch seems wrong, or the colour doesn't work, unpick the stitch.

Work the small rosebuds in Long and Short stitches and Satin stitch. To complete the embroidery, work clusters of French Knots in the centre of the full blooms, using the mustard-apricot-cinnamon range of colours. Work the stamens and pistils of the rosehips with several short Straight stitches radiating from the top of the hip, and clusters of French Knots to complete the effect. Use the same range of colours as you used for the rose centres.

Finishing
Remove the completed embroidery from the frame.

Making up the cushion
Cut the traced pattern on the broken line and pin the pattern to the embroidery, matching the design lines. Work basting stitches round the edge of the pattern. Unpin the pattern and cut out the cushion face, 1cm (⅜in) from the basted line. Baste the remaining wool and cotton fabric squares together and pin the pattern to the fabrics, cutting out the cushion back in the same way as for the cushion face.

Prepare the piping by machine-stitching the cord inside the binding. Pin, baste and then machine-stitch the piping round the cushion face on the seam line, matching the edges. Overlap the binding at the point of joining and hand-sew to neaten.

Place the cushion back on the embroidered cushion face, right sides facing, then pin, baste and machine-stitch all round, taking a 1cm (⅜in) seam and leaving a gap in the seam for inserting the cushion pad.

Clip into the curves to ease the seam and turn the cushion cover to the right side.

Use the paper pattern to cut the pillow ticking to the cushion shape. Sew two pieces of ticking together to make a cushion pad in the same way as the cushion cover was made and insert the filling. Close the opening with slip-stitches. Put the cushion pad inside the cushion cover and close the open seam with neat slip-stitches.

Other ideas for the design

The cushion has been successfully worked with woollen yarns but the design would look just as effective worked in pearl cotton or stranded cotton threads. The circlet of roses could also be interpreted into a canvaswork pattern. Copy the design onto squared paper, simplifying the shapes and colouring in squares. Worked in Tent stitch on canvas, the design would look superb worked on a stool top.

Trace-off pattern for the Double Dog Rose cushion; trace the half-section, then re-position the tracing paper to trace the other half, matching design lines

73

Rosa provincialis   *Blandford or Portugal Rose*

Blandford or Portugal Rose Sachet

The Blandford or Portugal Rose *Rosa provincialis* is believed to be of European origin but the date it first appeared in England is not known.

The daintiness of Mary Lawrance's drawing inspired a heart-shaped sachet and this has been worked in a combination of shadow work and surface stitchery.

In this project, the shadow effect is achieved by 'sandwiching' shapes cut from coloured fabrics between layers of organdie and cotton fabric.

Stitches
Back stitch, Straight stitch and French Knots.

Materials required
36cm (14in) square of white cotton organdie

36cm (14in) square of white cotton backing fabric
25cm (10in) square of pale green, pink, or floral fabric
small pieces of pale green, very pale green and pale pink cotton fabrics
50cm (20in) of 3mm (⅛in) rose pink satin ribbon
50cm (20in) of 3mm (⅛in) mint green satin ribbon
60cm (24in) of 1cm (⅜in) white lace edging
1 skein each of Madeira embroidery floss: 0102 (pale yellow); 0607 (very pale pink); 0613 (pale pink); 1702, 1309, 1310 (green)
white sewing thread
small amount of Terylene polyester filling (or other suitable filling)
pot pourri or lavender
water-soluble adhesive

Preparation
Trace both of the patterns on pages 76–77 onto tracing paper. Spray-starch and iron the pink and green fabrics. Use trace-off pattern A to trace the shapes on the pink and green fabrics. Use the very pale green for the larger leaves and the deeper green for the buds and smaller leaves. Cut out the shapes using sharp-pointed trimming scissors.

Place the white cotton backing fabric in a 25cm (10in) diameter embroidery hoop. Position this over trace-off pattern B and, using this as a guide, place the small cut-out shapes in position, using a little fabric adhesive to hold them to the backing fabric. Trace the curving stems from the pattern using a fabric-marking pencil.

Remove the backing fabric from the embroidery hoop, taking care not to disturb the glued-on shapes. Place the organdie over the backing fabric, smoothing the layers against one another, sandwiching the small cut shapes in place. Put the sandwiched fabrics back into the hoop.

Working the embroidery
Use three strands of embroidery thread throughout this design.

Work small, even-sized Back stitches round each fabric shape to hold them in position. Use the deepest green shade to work the large leaves and continue with this shade to work the leaf veins.

Use the two pale green threads to work the stems and round the shapes of the small leaves and buds. Try to balance the use of the two shades of green, and use them to work the thicker stems, working a third line of Back stitches in a deeper coloured green thread.

To make the sepals look more graceful as they split and unfurl to reveal the young rose petals, extend the line of Back stitches so that the shapes have very fine, pointed tips.

Use the deeper pink thread to work a few small, Straight stitch prickles on either side of the main stem. This deeper pink shade is also used to work the inner petals of the full bloom, and a few petals of the bloom seen from a side view.

Work the remaining petals of the full bloom and all the buds with the paler pink thread, keeping the stitches evenly sized. Work a few pale pink

Straight stitches on the very young buds where the petals are just beginning to emerge.

Finally, work a cluster of very pale green French Knots in the centre of the full bloom and then a circle of knots around the cluster.

Finishing

Remove the embroidery from the hoop and press it lightly on the wrong side to remove any creases.

Using the traced-off pattern, cut out a heart-shaped pattern. Pin this to the embroidery and baste round the pattern. Cut out, 1cm (⅜in) from the basting. Use the paper pattern to cut out the sachet backing. With right sides together, pin and baste the embroidery and backing together. Machine-stitch around the heart shape on the seam line, leaving an opening along a straight part of the heart shape for turning.

Clip into the curved seam allowance and turn the sachet to the right side. Stuff the sachet with filling and insert the pot pourri or lavender deep into the middle of the sachet. Close the opening with invisible slip-stitches.

Hand-sew the narrow lace edging round the sachet folding the ends under to conceal the join.

Tie the pink and green ribbons into a double bow and hand-sew the bow at the top of the heart.

Trace-off shapes for the shadow work (A)

76

Trace-off pattern for the Portugal Rose sachet (B)

Rosa carolina

Upright Carolina Rose

Upright Carolina Rose Towel

The Upright Carolina Rose *Rosa carolina* is a beautiful example of this species. The rose is a native of North America and is noted for the colour change in the leaves in autumn which turn red and yellow before they drop.

Because the rose has an 'old-fashioned' look, it was decided to use the flower for traditional house linen – the huckaback guest towel. Pure linen towels are hard-wearing and long-lasting and the time spent in embroidery is thus rewarded with years of use. The spray abstracted from Mary Lawrance's drawing has been used to work the ends of towels and a smaller spray of rosehips and buds is given for matching accessories.

The rosehips in this design add an extra point of interest because hips are not present in many of the designs in this book.

The stitches used in this project are simple but must be worked carefully if they are to have the desired effect. They are worked directly onto the huckaback linen fabric and this will not be lined so it is important to finish thread ends neatly on the wrong side.

Stitches
Blanket stitch, Chain stitch, Straight stitch and French Knots.

Materials required
To make two guest towels

2 pure Irish linen huckaback guest towels

1 skein each of Anchor stranded embroidery cotton: 311 (pale orange); 292 (pale yellow) for stamens and pistil; 266, 216 (deep greens) for leaves; 214, 264 (pale greens) for leaves, sepals, stems of hips and buds; 896 (deep pink) for

thorns; 76, 36, 893 (pinks) for the petals.

Preparation

Trace the rose spray patterns on page 81.

You may find that with a good, strong light over the area of work you will be able to trace the design straight through onto the linen fabric. If you can see the design, use this method to transfer the rose spray onto the centre of one end of the towel. However, if you do not feel confident enough to do this, use an embroidery transfer pencil to trace the design onto a sheet of tracing paper. Remember the design will become reversed if you do this, but in this case it will not really detract from the success of your stitchery.

Follow the instructions supplied with the pencil to transfer the design onto the towel. Place the area to be embroidered in a 20cm (8in) diameter hoop, re-positioning it during embroidery as necessary.

Working the embroidery

Use three strands of embroidery thread throughout this design.

Work the darker leaves and stems first. You will see from the picture of the towel that there are three stems of dark leaves, one group coming out from behind the centre bloom and then a Chain stitch stem curves to the left and to the right of this bloom. Each leaf is worked in two sections using Blanket stitch and is then linked to a Chain stitch stem. One side of the leaf is worked in the same colour as the stem and the other side in the alternative dark green. Blanket stitches should be evenly worked with a small space between the stitches; they slant away from the centre vein of the leaf so that the graceful shape is emphasised.

Work the remaining large leaves in the same way, using the two paler shades of green. Again using these pale green threads, work the gently curving stems with tiny Chain stitches. Where these stems develop into small leaves, open out the Chain stitches to go across the width of the leaves and close up the stitch at the points of the leaves.

The sepals are similarly worked in Chain and Open Chain stitches, while the bulbous part of the buds and hips are worked in two sections using Blanket stitch, in the same way as the leaves were formed.

The rose petals in this design have been interpreted with Blanket stitch outlining. The petals have not been filled as the strength of the outlined shape is sufficient to give them identity. When working these, balance the use of the pink shades so that the darker pink is on the outside of the flowers. This shade is also used to work the petals that are just visible in the rosebuds. Work a few small Straight stitches along the two dark green stems, using deep pink thread to represent thorns.

Finally, using a single strand of pale green thread, work several short Straight stitches around the centre of the full bloom and work more at the ends of the rose hips. Using pale orange, work small French Knots in the centre of the full bloom. Use the same colour to work clusters of Knots on the hips.

Work clusters of pale orange Knots round the Straight stitches in the full bloom.

Finishing

Remove the embroidery from the hoop. Steam-press lightly on the wrong side. If desired, spray-starch can be used to crispen the towel.

Small spray motif

A smaller spray pattern is given on page 81, or alternatively the motif shown below could be used. This is provided for matching items which may require a smaller motif.

Other ideas for the design

The matching patterns could be used for a set of place mats and napkins or, if the larger spray were set at the ends of a long, rectangular cloth, either of the smaller sprays might be set along the sides.

This design would translate prettily into other embroidery techniques, such as embroidery on tulle for a bridal veil, or the motif could be used in white on white for bridal clothes. The small, individual motif is an ideal size for small accessories, such as an embroidered book cover.

Trace-off pattern for alternative matching motif

Matching motif for the Upright Carolina Rose embroidery

Trace-off pattern used on the huckaback towel

Rosa provincialis   *Rose de Meaux*

Rose de Meaux Panel

The Rose de Meaux *Rosa provincalis* is thought to have come from the garden of Dominique Seguier, Bishop of Meaux, around 1637, who was a keen rose grower. It is similar to a cabbage rose in shape but a miniature and smaller in every way.

The bright pink rose has inspired a wall panel worked in persian wool, similar to crewel wool, but slightly thicker. The design could also be used to work a cushion cover, or in stranded embroidery cotton the motif is suitable for table linens.

Stitches
Satin stitch variations, Stem stitch, French Knots and Sheaf stitch.

Materials required
50cm (20in) square of white cotton or linen coarse-weave fabric
50cm (20in) white cotton backing fabric
80cm (31in) of 1cm (⅜in) green velvet ribbon
114cm (45in) of 1cm (⅜in) dusty pink velvet ribbon
1 skein each of Paterna persian wool yarn: 436 (light chocolate brown); 664 (pale pine green); 962 (bright hot pink); 963 (pale hot pink)
2 skeins each of Paterna persian wool yarn: 964 (very pale hot pink); 614 (very pale hunter green)
sewing thread to match velvet ribbons
40cm (16in) square of white mounting card
50cm (20in) square of tracing paper

Preparation
Trace the patterns on pages 84–85 using a fabric transfer pencil.

Place the two fabrics together, edges matching, and baste them together. Stretch the mounted fabric onto a rectangular or square frame. Following the manufacturer's instructions for the transfer pencil, transfer the design to the fabric, including the broken lines which indicate the ribbon borders. Repositioning the pattern, transfer the corner motifs (see pictured panel).

Working the embroidery
Lay the ribbons, so that the outer edge aligns with the broken guide lines. Sew the green velvet ribbon along the inner guide lines and the dusty pink ribbon along the outer guide lines. Fold the corners to give a sharp, mitred look. Sew the ribbons using matching threads and making small prick stitches along both edges.

Work the space between the borders in a pattern of Sheaf stitches, using very pale hunter green and very pale hot pink wool. Work the stitches in a random pattern. This decorative stitchery links the colouring of the velvet ribbons with the foliage and petals of the Rose de Meaux design and also creates an interesting area of texture. The four corner sprays and the central design are worked in built-up Satin stitch together with Stem stitch and a few carefully positioned French Knots. Work the leaves in two sections, in Satin stitch, using the two shades of green. Lay stitches close together so that a solid area of texture and colour is formed. Unite the two sides of the leaves with gently curving Stem stitching for the veins. Similarly, the pale brown stems of the rosebuds are worked in Stem stitch. Where the stems broaden out at the base of the buds gradually change your stitches into Satin stitch, and the colouring from brown to green. As you work up towards the bud tip, the sepals are more effective if worked in several closely-spaced lines of Stem stitch. Fill in the small areas with pale hot pink Satin stitch to make it appear as if the petals are about to unfurl.

The single slightly larger and more mature bud in the centre design has pale hot pink petals emerging from the sepals, as well as bright hot pink petals.

Work the full blooms of the centre design and the corner sprays by building up the petals in the graded shades of pink so that the palest shade lies on the edges of the petals and the deepest pink shade lies towards the

base end of each petal, or towards the centre of the bloom. Look closely at the panel and compare it with the trace-off pattern to see how the shapes have been interpreted into colour and stitch and this will help your embroidery.

Complete the flowers with a few small French Knots to represent the pistil and stamens and also to make a focal point in each flower. Work the scattered groups of tiny stylised stamens around the outside of the design in pale pine green Stem stitch, with light chocolate brown French Knots for the heads.

Finishing

Remove the fabric from the embroidery frame. Stretch and lace it over the piece of strong, white mounting card, keeping the lines of ribbon straight and square.

Frame the stretched and mounted embroidery.

Trace this corner motif onto the fabric four
times

Trace-off pattern and guide lines for the Rose
de Meaux panel. Match the two sections on the
design lines

Rosa pendulina   *Rose Without Thorns*

Rose Without Thorns Picture

The Rose Without Thorns *Rosa pendulina* has an uncertain origin and, in her book, Mary Lawrance suggests that it may have been a native of Spain or Italy. Records show that it was grown in England in 1726 by James Sherard MD, as a species rose (not a hybrid) and the Kew catalogue entry of 1789 indicates the rose was in the Gardens at that time.

The drawing by Mary Lawrance has been interpreted almost exactly into a Cross stitched picture worked on Hardanger fabric in the true colours. The unusual, crimson-tinged stems, for instance, are faithfully reproduced in reddish-brown thread. The leaves of the Rose are prominent in the original drawing and the interpretation similarly gives the leaves emphasis in the embroidery.

Working chart for the Rose Without Thorns picture. Each square of the chart represents one Cross stitch worked over two vertical and two horizontal threads.

Stitches
Cross stitch.

Materials required
50×60cm (20×24in) white
  Hardanger fabric, 9 threads per cm
  (22 threads per in)
1 skein each of Anchor stranded
  cotton: 307 (deep gold); 305 (pale
  gold); 48 (very pale pink); 50 (pale
  pink); 40 (cyclamen pink); 26
  (cherry pink); 213 (very pale
  willow); 216 (deep willow); 264
  (yellow-green); 267 (deep grass
green); 263 (dark forest green); 352 (dark rust brown); 21 (very dark brown); 1 (white)
contrasting sewing thread
mounting card

Preparation
Trim the fabric to size, cutting carefully along thread lines. Neaten the fabric edges with oversewing or zigzag machine-stitching.

Count threads along the top and down one side to find the middle point. Work basting threads vertically and horizontally to mark the exact centre of the fabric.

The picture can be worked in a frame or in the hand but if you decide to work without a frame, care must be taken to see that stitch tension is even throughout.

Working the embroidery
Use three strands of embroidery cotton throughout this design.

Using a fine, blunt-tipped tapestry needle, work the picture in Cross stitch, following the colour chart and key to colours on page 83. Each square on the chart represents one Cross stitch, worked over two vertical and two horizontal threads. Work from the centre outwards, remembering to make all the top threads of the Cross stitches lie in the same direction. This is important to obtain the neat, even look that is characteristic of Cross stitch.

It is often easier to work a complete shape – for example, a leaf in which several colours are used – before moving on to the next section, rather than trying to move from one area of the design to another using the same colour. It is easy to jump a square and cause the design to become distorted. Try to keep the wrong side of the work as neat as possible, weaving thread ends into the back of stitches,

Key

▨	307	▨	264
☐	305	▨	267
▨	48	▨	263
▨	50	▨	352
▨	40	▨	21
■	26	▨	1
▨	213	▨	216

and trimming ends neatly so that loose ends do not show through at the front of the work.

Finishing
When the embroidery is completed, unpick the vertical and horizontal basting threads. If the embroidery has been worked without a frame, it will almost certainly need pressing. Place the embroidery right side down on a pad of several layers of clean, colour-fast fabric (several tea towels will do). Pressing over a soft pad encourages the embroidery threads to become more pronounced. Press gently with a steam iron, or with a dry iron on top of a damp cloth.

Mounting embroidery for framing
Embroidery must be mounted on heavy card before framing. Cut the card to fit your frame. Place the embroidery face down on a flat surface and put the card on the back, exactly centred. Fold the fabric edges onto the card and push pins into the card edges to hold the fabric. Mitre the corners neatly. Thread a tapestry needle with doubled button thread and work long lacing stitches, from side to side and from top to bottom, through the fabric edges. Remove the pins.

Other ways of using the design
The chart on page 87 can be used to work the picture on canvas, using tapisserie wools. Either Cross stitch, Tent stitch or Half Cross stitch could be used, or a selection of other textured stitches might be considered. The finished size of the canvaswork can be estimated by counting the number of squares across the top and down one side of the chart and dividing these numbers by the number of threads per cm or inch in your selected canvas.

Working chart for the Rose Without Thorns picture
Each square of the chart represents one Cross stitch worked over two vertical and two horizontal threads in the fabric.

A Garden of Roses

The trace-off patterns on this and the following pages are designed from the roses drawn by Mary Lawrance. They will provide an almost limitless collection of embroidery motifs which can be adapted, enlarged, reduced, linked etc and from which individual motifs can be abstracted. Use them with the Mary Lawrance drawings to create your own original embroideries.

The art of embroidering flowers

The most important factor in flower embroidery can only be achieved with a practised and discerning eye, an awareness of the effect of light on the colour and texture of a living flower and its interpretation into fabric and thread. The senses – sight, touch and smell – are all used when appreciating a flower. Similarly, sight and touch are used in appreciating the gentle art of embroidery.

Begin by deciding the effect you wish to achieve and the purpose of the embroidered article. With these factors in mind, you are ready to choose fabrics and threads, and to decide the techniques which will enable you to fulfil your design idea. The patterns on this and following pages use certain design 'recipes'. For example, a spray of roses may be so designed that it can be repeated to border a curtain or edge a tablecloth. By studying the spray you may also be able to abstract a single rose with leaves, or a group of buds, and use the design in isolation on table napkins or perhaps on pillow cases.

Similarly, you will see that some of the sprays are balanced on either side of a central bloom with identical, but reversed components. When you are abstracting parts of a design for a specific use, try this 'recipe' and you will see how effective it can be. Trace off several different blooms, rosebuds and leaf stalks, cut them out and try different arrangements on a sheet of paper until you have a design that pleases you. Fix the pieces in place with a little adhesive and then re-trace

the motifs to produce your own, original embroidery pattern.

All the patterns here, and on previous pages, can be enlarged in size, or reduced for smaller motifs, but always review the new size critically before starting to embroider. While the proportions remain the same, the new size may not be so pleasing. Enlarged shapes can easily become clumsy while a reduction in size can sometimes produce a fussy effect, or simply become too difficult to handle in stitchery.

Choosing stitches

If you look through the various projects on previous pages, you will see that only a few stitches have been used to work the embroideries. They are all popular, well-known stitches and each has been selected to achieve an effect. While you may enjoy experimenting with different stitches – and there are hundreds to choose from – you do not need a full repertoire to interpret flowers into embroidery. The art lies in perfect execution, suitability for the final use of the embroidered article and the colours you choose to work with.

A Stitch Library of the stitches used in this book is provided on pages 92–94.

Rose Without Thorns *This spray could be used singly on cushions or place mats but could also be adapted to make a repeat motif.*

Alpine Rose *A simple circlet for a tablecloth centre, or for an embroidered bed cover. The circlet could also be used for a trolley cloth or a traycloth.*

Marbled Scotch Rose *A small single motif such as this can be used singly, on items such as table napkins, or grouped on tablecloths or bed linens.*

Stepney Rose *Use this single motif as a small picture, or perhaps for an embroidered book cover. Single motifs can also be used to work special gift cards for anniversaries.*

Double Dog Rose *Use this garland for a towel edging, or for a tie-back. It could also be repeated as a 'scallop' design to edge a tablecloth or a bed cover.*

STITCH LIBRARY

Back Stitch

Bring the thread through on the stitch line, then take a small backward stitch through the fabric. Bring the needle through again a little in front of the first stitch, take another stitch, inserting the needle at the point where it first came through.

Blanket Stitch and Buttonhole Stitch

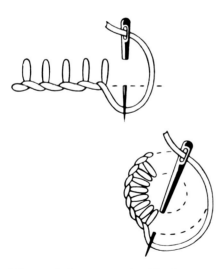

These stitches are worked in the same way – the difference being that in Buttonhole Stitch the stitches are close together. Bring the thread out on the lower line, insert the needle in position in the upper line, taking a straight downward stitch with the thread under the needle point. Pull up the stitch to form a loop and repeat.

Bullion Knots

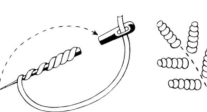

Pick up a Back Stitch, the size of the Bullion Knot required, bringing the needle point out where it first emerged; do not pull the needle right through the fabric. Twist the thread round the needle point as many times as required to equal the space of the Back Stitch. Hold the left thumb on the coiled thread and pull the needle through; still holding the coiled thread, turn the needle back to where it was inserted (see arrow) and insert in same place. Pull thread through until the Bullion Knot lies flat. Use a needle with a small eye to allow the thread to pass through the coils easily.

Chain Stitch

Bring the thread out at the top of the line and hold down with left thumb. Insert the needle where it last emerged and bring the point out a short distance away. Pull the thread through, keeping the working thread under the needle point.

Closed Herringbone Stitch

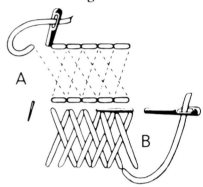

This stitch is used for Shadow Work on fine transparent fabric and can be worked on the right side of the fabric as Fig A – a small Back Stitch worked alternately on each side of the traced double lines (the dotted lines on the diagram show the formation of the thread on the wrong side of the fabric). The colour of the thread appears delicately through the fabric. Fig B shows the stitch worked on the wrong side of the fabric as a Closed Herringbone Stitch with no spaces left between the stitches. Both methods achieve the same result.

Cross Stitch

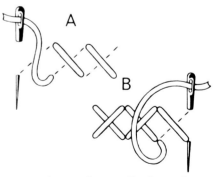

Fig A – bring the needle through on the lower right line of the cross and insert at the top of the same line, taking a stitch through the fabric to lower left line. Continue to the end of the row in this way. Fig B – complete the other half of the cross. It is important that the upper half of each stitch lies in one direction.

Fishbone Stitch

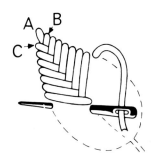

Long and Short Stitch

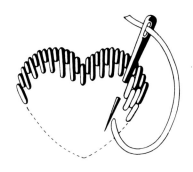

Roumanian Couching

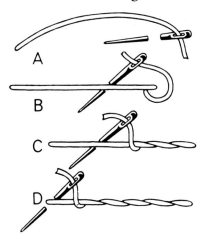

This stitch is useful for filling small shapes. Bring the thread through at A and make a small straight stitch along the centre line of the shape. Bring the thread through again at B and make a sloping stitch across the central line at the base of the first stitch. Bring the thread through at C and make a similar sloping stitch to overlap the previous stitch. Continue working alternately on each side until the shape is filled.

This form of Satin Stitch is so named as all the stitches are of varying lengths. It is often used to fill a shape which is too large or too irregular to be covered by Satin Stitch. It is also used to achieve a shaded effect. In the first row the stitches are alternately long and short and closely follow the outline of the shape. The stitches in the following rows are worked to achieve a smooth appearance. The diagram shows how a shaded effect may be obtained.

This form of couching is useful for filling in large spaces in which a flat indefinite background is required. Bring the thread through on the left, carry the thread across the space to be filled and take a small stitch on the right with the thread above the needle (A). Take small stitches along the line at intervals, as in B and C, to the end of the laid thread, emerging in position for the next stitch (D).

Satin Stitch

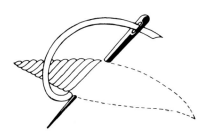

French Knots

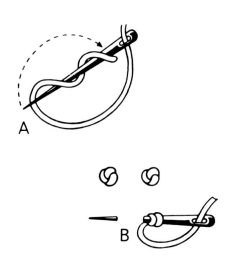

Overcast Stitch

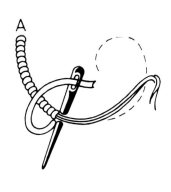

Work Straight Stitches closely together across the shape, as shown in the diagram; care must be taken to keep a good edge. Do not made the stitches too long, as they would then be liable to be pulled out of position.

Seeding

Bring the thread out at the required position, hold the thread down with the left thumb and encircle the thread twice with the needle as at A. Still holding the thread firmly, twist the needle back to the starting point and insert it close to where the thread first emerged (see arrow). Pull thread through to the back and secure for a single French Knot or pass on to the position of the next stitch as at B.

Bring the laid threads through at A and hold with left thumb, then bring through the working thread at A and work small Satin Stitches closely over the laid threads, following the line of the design. The laid threads are taken through to the back of the fabric to finish. This stitch resembles a fine cord and is useful for embroidering delicate stems and outlines.

This simple filling stitch is composed of small Straight Stitches of equal length placed at random over the surface, as shown on the diagram.

Sheaf Stitch

An attractive filling stitch consisting of three vertical Satin Stitches tied across the centre with two horizontal Overcasting Stitches. The Overcasting Stitches are worked round the Satin Stitches, the needle only entering the fabric to pass on to the next sheaf. The sheaves may be worked in alternate rows as shown, or in close horizontal rows directly below each other.

Straight Stitch (also known as Single Satin Stitch)

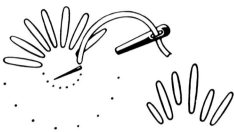

This is shown as single spaced stitches worked either in a regular or irregular manner. Sometimes the stitches are of varying size; they should be neither too long nor too loose.

Split Stitch

Bring the thread through at A and make a small stitch over the line of the design, piercing the working thread with the needle as shown in the diagram. Split Stitch may be used as a filling where a fine flat surface is required.

Stem Stitch

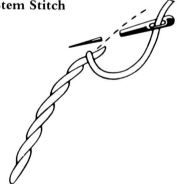

Work from left to right, taking regular, small stitches along the line of the design. The thread always emerges on the left side of the previous stitch. The stitch is used for flower stems, outlines etc. It can also be used as a filling with rows of Stem Stitch worked closely together.

Single Yellow Rose *A single rose and leaf spray which could make a framed picture.*

BIBLIOGRAPHY

CREDITS

Blunt, Wilfrid. *The New Naturalist: The Art of Botanical Illustration* (Collins, 1950)
Farington, Joseph, RA. *The Farington Diary, edited by James Grieg* (Hutchison, 1922)
Gibson, M. *The Book of the Rose* London (MacDonald General Books 1980)
Graves, Algernon, FSA. *The Royal Academy of Arts. A Complete Dictionary of contributors and their work from its foundation in 1769 to 1904* (Graves, 1905)
Harkness, Jack. *Roses*. London (J. M. Dent & Sons Ltd. 1978)
Krüssmann, G. *The Complete Book of Roses*, Portland, Oregon (Timber Press 1981)
Mallalieu, H. L. *The Dictionary of British Watercolour Artists up to 1920* (Antique Collectors' Club, 1976)
Ray, Desmond. *Dictionary of British and Irish Botanists and Horticulturists Including Plant Collectors and Botanical Artists* (Taylor & Francis, 1977)
Redgrave, Samuel. *A Dictionary of Artists of the English School* (Longmans, 1874)
Thomas, G. S. *The Old Shrub Roses*. London (J. M. Dent & Sons Ltd. 1979)
Willmott, Ellen, FLS. *The Genus Rosa Volume I* (J. Murray, 1914)

The author and the publishers are grateful to the following companies which supplied materials for the projects in the book.
Coats Patons Crafts for stranded embroidery cotton, coton perlé and Tapisserie wool.
The stitches on pages 85–87 are reproduced by kind permission of J. & P. Coats Limited, and are taken from their booklet *100 Embroidery Stitches*.
DMC Threads for stranded embroidery cotton, coton perlé, coton à broder, Medicis Laine.
Habitat Designs Limited for fabrics.
Madeira Threads (UK) Limited for embroidery floss.
Paterna for Persian wool yarns.
C. M. Offray & Son Limited for ribbons.

INDEX